NANAK

An Introduction

To

The lore of Ten Nanaks

That inspired me as nothing else did

NANAK
An Introduction

Purushottam Nijhaawan

Vakils, Feffer and Simons Private Ltd.
Hague Building, 9, Sprott Road, Ballard Estate,
Mumbai 400 001. India

First printing 2004

Price in India Rs. 295/-

Published by Bimal Mehta
for Vakils, Feffer and Simons Private Ltd.
Hague Building, 9, Sprott Road, Ballard Estate
Mumbai 400 001. India

Printed by Arun K. Mehta at Vakil & Sons Private Ltd.
Industry Manor, Appasaheb Marathe Marg
Worli, Mumbai 400 025. India

ISBN 81-87111-67-4

Contents

Cover:

Donning the Baghdadi *Choga*, Nanak at the height of his world conquest. This *Choga* has the *Ayats* of the holy Quran calligraphed on it. One such *Choga* is still preserved at Dera Baba Nanak.

Acknowledgements

I am deeply grateful to the following:

Prof. Dalip Singh, formerly of the Khalsa College Mumbai, and a profound scholar of Nanak and Sikhism for graciously acting as my resource person;

The late Raja Sir Daljit Singh of the house of Kapurthala for using all the *Janam Sakhi* material from his profound work "Guru Nanak", at places even verbatim, because I let it remain as it is as my humble tribute to the original author;

Sardar Swinder Singh Sahni, Chairman of the *Dharma Prachar* Committee, Singh Sabha, Dadar, Mumbai for his help and assistance in illustrating it.

Parag Borse for creating some beautiful illustrations to support the contents of the text;

Dr. Sangat Singh for all the historical information and material;

Miss Usha Bhatia of the Lalit Kala Akademi Govt. of India for her general advice and help.

My son, Amit Kapoor for critically improving the text;

Mr. Arun K. Mehta of Vakils, Feffer and Simons Private Ltd., Mumbai, for giving me the opportunity to do this book;

And finally, my editor Pallavi Guptaa who made this book what it is.

About this Book

Nanak and Sikhism cannot be separated from each other. In fact, Sikhism is nothing but Nanak in practice. Hence, we shall deal with the entire subject as Nanak only. The beauty of it is that Nanak or his manifestation the Sikh Church is assuming even greater dimension as it is growing and evolving. And it is this aspect that we have tried to highlight more than anything else. For, it makes Nanak universal.

Even so, the book seeks to study Nanak as Ten Nanaks and lastly as eternal Nanak in whom each Sikh finds himself in the immanent protection of his Guru. Perhaps our fugitive world needs nothing better than this to be able to cope with the multifarious challenges of today and tomorrow. The Prologue and the Epilogue in the main help us understand this aspect.

Happily, there is nothing pedantic about either Nanak or Sikhism. Both are a living lore of Punjab. They sprang up from the soil, as it were, as a spiritual faith of unimaginable proportions. Thus, only simple tools are needed to understand them as they grew from stage to stages.

We have divided the subject matter into ten chapters to see how one aspect flows out of the other in a natural way. Besides, the book is suitably illustrated to help even the uninitiated to grasp the real import.

To add further value to this introduction, the Annexure One contains the English rendition of the *Japuji* as Nanak's unrivalled prayer for the entire humanity. It is accompanied by the original Punjabi text of the *Japuji* and its Devanagari transliteration. Those interested in knowing Nanak's wondrous God and his own philosophy of the **Nam** will it is hoped, immensely enjoy reading it.

Prologue

Nanak: A Special Spark of Divinity

The basic point about Nanak is that though very much a historical person, he happens to transcend the limitations that history imposes upon man. He became a legend of impossible proportions in his own lifetime. Thus, any introduction of him has to draw upon material that's much larger than life. His persona and achievements can, therefore, only be culled out from a mixture of history, legends, myths and miracles that developed around him.

That also explains how Nanak became the subject of a vast hagiographic literature known as *Janam Sakhi*s. And this literature contains his gospel in the language of symbols, allegories, allusions and parables. However, it as well reveals the basic contours of his life and times. In fact, these *Sakhi*s alone give the necessary context and perspective to his *Bani* or divine poetry that fills every moment of his extremely multifaceted life. Hence, linear history, as we know, is a poor substitute for knowing Nanak, the purpose of this volume.

Who is the Nanak of the *Janam Sakhi*s? "*Miti Dhund Jag Chanan Howa*" was how Bhai Gurdas, the first accredited chronicler of the Nanak lore, hailed his birth. Translated it means, "Melted the mist (of sham and hypocrisy) and filled was the world with sunshine (of faith and hope)." Perhaps this is how all the '*Messiahs*' of the world have been hailed through the ages. But Nanak is unique even among them. He is not only the very last of them but has also admirably integrated the totality of their wisdom into a universal message — all his own.

And it underscores all the three points that most men and women, curious about religion, are most likely to ask: (1) What are the conditions when God sends his own spark or messiah to the earth?; (2) how does the messiah then redeem God's covenant with man?; and (3) what is it that he leaves behind to sustain his noble mission of spiritual regeneration? We have endeavoured to familiarize the inquisitive on all the three points.

As to the first point, Lord Krishna has clearly underlined the principle in His 'Song Celestial'. The principle is, "Whenever *Dharma* — the divine imperative of being and becoming — goes under and *Adharma*, the negation of that imperative, becomes all pervasive, I (God) incarnate myself".

Not just that, the Lord further promises that it shall happen age after age and aeon after aeon. Now when we apply this irrevocable promise of the Lord to Nanak, we discover its verity. Nanak was God's own intervention to re-establish the universal moral order that was then rapidly vanishing.

It was no easy task. The age in which Nanak was born had badly divided both God and man. Men were engaged in dividing God and He, in turn, was doing the same to men. The main casualty was the sacredness of life. It is to this challenge that Nanak addressed himself.

To accomplish this onerous task, he took nine rebirths and then became immanent to his Sikhs in the form of the Word God, thus laying the foundation of Sikhism, a uniquely corporate religion of the world. This way Nanak not only resurrected himself nine times but also became eternally relevant to the spiritual needs of man in this ever-changing world.

This task is by no means finished. The challenge of God dividing men and the vice versa happening exists in much worse form today. In his own time, Nanak had proclaimed the oneness of Ram of the Hindus and Rahim of the Muslims with unique success. But today Mohammed's Allah and Christ's Lord must also become one if humanity must survive. Hence, Nanak appears to be even more relevant now. For, his message alone has the potential of proclaiming the spiritual unity of God and man. Nanak's God is common to all, to every particle of creation.

In practical terms, Nanak was forthright in attacking the life of escape, austerity, superstition, ritual, doubt, guile and duplicity. He advocated avoiding all extremes to follow the middle path. He established the truth by telling people to earn their living the hard, honest way and share it with the have-nots.

He also asked seekers to constantly remember God through the *Nam* and live by His *Reza* or *Hukum* (will or direction) i.e. the inner voice. Nanak's *Wahe* Guru or God is full of immense grace and solicitude for the suffering humanity. No wonder then, he succeeded in creating such heroic and saintly men, making history at every step.

In short, Nanak is a spiritual revolutionary par excellence. His very touch transformed a sick and moribund society into a dynamic and vital force in no time. In the form of Sikhism, he created an instrument that combined modernity with tradition and change with permanence. That's why his revolution has proved far more enduring than most historical revolutions.

Also, in Nanak's path both men and women are uniquely equal and spiritual, and much above any gender bias. This makes the family a unit of society where God and his divinity dwell. "*Ghar Vich Udas*" is Nanak's cardinal status, which means all detachment must flow from commitment.

In the end, while Nanak attaches utmost importance to truth, he rates 'truthful living' as of far higher purpose than truth itself. Thus, in every situation, he seems to opt for the practical than the abstract.

Nanak's Uncommon Early Years   Chapter I

Guru Nanak was born at Talwandi Rai Bhoeki, now Nankana Sahib, in Pakistan in 1469 AD in the home of his maternal grandfather. His traditional date of birth is the full moon day of the month of *Kartik* that corresponds to the months of October and November of the Gregorian calendar. However, most scholars now place his date of birth as April 15 — the date as mentioned in the *Janam Sakhi* of Meharvan.

His father's name was Mehta Kalyan Chand Bedi who was also called Mehta Kalu Rai or simply Kalu. He was the village revenue accountant or *Patwari*, and owned some agricultural land in the village. So, he was comparatively well off and influential. His mother's name was Tripta, a self-effacing woman. Nanak also had a sister named Nanaki, several years his elder. So, for the most part, Nanak was the only child his parents doted over.

From the *Janam Sakhi*s we know that Nanak was a chubby and winsome child whom one could also call a 'chosen one'. For, after seeing him, the Hindus would say, "Great is Gobind, the Lord. Such a young child and yet he speaks so sweetly. He is truly in the image of God Himself." Similarly, on beholding him, the Muslims would observe, "Wonderful is thy creation, O Merciful. See this child. It looks as if he is blessed by Allah Himself."

However, very little information is available as to what kind of child Nanak was. All we know is that he lay calmly in the cradle, seldom crying. He always seemed to gaze

The famous Nankana Sahib Gurdwara. Guru Nanak was born at Talwandi Rai Bheoki, later renamed as Nankana.

Child Nanak perplexes the Pandit at *Pathshala* (the temple school) on the very first day of receiving lessons by forming the word '*Soi*', meaning the creator of the universe.

upwards, trying to read something in the sky that eluded others. And when he learnt to walk, he generally avoided playing with other children of his age. Most of the time, he would keep indoors, lost in contemplation. All in all, he was a very precocious and inward-looking child.

Father sends Nanak to the *Pathshala*

At the age of seven, Kalu sent him to the village Pandit with due ceremonies. His first lesson was to form words connecting alphabets. Nanak took the slate and sat in a corner, joining the letters. Soon, Nanak informed the Pandit that he had formed a word. "What's it?" the Pandit asked. Nanak promptly said it was '*soi*'. The Pandit was perplexed and asked what '*soi*' meant. Without a second thought, Nanak said, '*soi*' meant the One who has created this universe. The Pandit was completely floored. What could he teach a child like Nanak? There is also a poem included in the Sri Guru Granth Sahib, supposed to have been authored by the young Nanak. Each verse of this poem starts with a letter of the Gurmukhi alphabet. Such poems are called acrostics. This poem reflects upon questions far beyond the years of Nanak.

The Thread Ceremony

At the age of 11, Nanak was to be given the sacred thread. This ceremony is equivalent to a baptismal, conferring upon the high-caste Hindu boys a spiritual rebirth. They are then called *dwija*s and are deemed fit to perform all religious ceremonies as also to go to the Guru's home for higher studies. This is an important family and religious ritual that all the clansmen are expected to attend.

After going through the preliminary ritual, the priest got ready to place the sacred thread around Nanak's shoulders. But before he could do so, Nanak stopped him. He wanted to know the significance of the cotton thread. He asked the priest, "Who makes this thread? Does it not decay? How does it absorb spiritual power?" These questions completely floored the learned Pandit. He could not come up with any convincing answer. As Nanak was not satisfied, he refused to proceed with his thread ceremony.

In the end, Nanak sang a hymn that invested the metaphor of the thread with its true significance. Some of its lines are like this:

Nanak refuses to accept the cotton thread from the family *Purohit* when the latter fails to explain the true significance of the thread ceremony.

> "Out of the cotton of compassion
> Spin the thread of contentment,
> Tie knots of continence and give it the twist of truth.
> Make such a sacred thread for the mind
> As once worn will never break
> Nor get soiled, burnt or lost.
> The man who wears such a thread is blessed."

This story makes two very significant points: One, Nanak was against rituals from the very start; and two, he could easily tell the real significance of things, investing old metaphors with new nuances.

Small Miracles of His Grace

There are some more stories signifying that Nanak was God's beloved from the very start. One story relates to how one day Rai Bular, the landlord of the village, found Nanak sleeping under the hot sun and noticed how the shadow of the tree under which he slept did not move like the shadows of other trees did with the sun's movement. This was enough for Rai Bular to conclude that Nanak was a child who reflected the glory of God. On another occasion, Rai Bular saw a king cobra spreading its hood on the sleeping Nanak while his cattle grazed in the fields. When he tried to save Nanak, the cobra silently slithered away. A smiling Nanak greeted him instead. Nanak would often take the cattle for grazing. One day, while he was in deep meditation, the cattle strayed into a neighbour's field and trampled over the blooming crop. When the farmer saw it, he not only reprimanded Nanak but also took the matter to Rai Bular. He wanted Mehta Kalu to compensate him for the loss.

Rai Bular sent an appraiser with the complainant so that the actual loss could be assessed. But when they arrived on the scene, they found the fields abloom with crops. The farmer had experienced his first miracle.

A king-cobra spreading his hood to protect the sleeping Nanak from the sun. In the old Indian tradition, it signifies that the child is a spark of divinity.

3

An Unusual Adolescence

As Nanak was growing up, Mehta Kalu was getting more and more worried that Nanak was not amenable to anything that could make him a man of the world. His mother had begun to worry too. Her friends lost no opportunity passing remarks about her growing son. The general refrain was that though Nanak looked normal, he was surely under the spell of an evil eye. This pained his mother.

One day she saw a group of *Sadhu*s pass along the street and felt a sudden twinge in her heart. When she shared the thought with her son that one day he too would leave her and roam about like these anchorites, Nanak assured her that he would never do as these *Sadhu*s did because his philosophy did not permit him. He explained to her that all impurities could be washed away even while leading a normal life at home, and that one did not have to abandon home and family in search of spiritual quest.

Physician! Heal Thyself

Nanak continued to remain indoors, making the prognostications of the people around seem true. So, finally Kalu summoned a physician named Hari Das to treat and, if possible, cure him of his strange malady. When the physician felt Nanak's pulse, Nanak spoke, "You are no

Nanak reassuring the physician that there was nothing wrong with his health and it was the physician who needed to look within to heal himself.

physician for you know not the pain that is buried in the heart. How can you act as a physician when you cannot remove your own pain?"

"What's my disease and what are its symptoms?" asked the physician totally surprised.

"You suffer from I-amness and that separates you from your fellowmen as well as from God."

"I am not concerned with I-amness. I cure physical ailments," he said.

At that, Nanak sang a hymn. The physician had never heard anything like it before.

> *"Man's mind binds with desires and sows the seeds*
>   *of its own suffering.*
> *In pursuit of indulgence of self, it forgets God and*
>   *gets endless suffering.*
> *O ignorant physician! Your body is of no avail.*
> *Suffering itself is the symptom of the disease as*
>   *also its cure."*

After gathering his wits, Hari Das, the physician turned to Mehta Kalu and said, "Your anxiety about your son is misplaced."

Some More Worldly Suggestions

Become a Farmer

Kalu tried every trick in the trade that a father sometimes has to. But to each one Nanak had a ready answer. For example, when Kalu suggested that Nanak should become a farmer, he forthwith said, "I am all the time engaged in real farming." And then he sang,

> *"This body is the field; the mind the ploughman.*
> *Using modesty as the irrigating water*
> *I sow the seed of Divine **Nam**.*
> *Then with the leveller of contentment*
> *I pulverize the crust of pride into true humility.*
> *In it shall prosper the seed of love.*
> *Seated in the abode of truth, I behold its progress."*

Become a Shopkeeper

However, after some days, Kalu again mustered courage to suggest that Nanak might think of becoming a shopkeeper.

Without even a second thought, Nanak sang forth,

> *"I make the frail body my shop.*
> *I make meditation my container.*
> *I stock my shop with true **Nam**;*
> *I trade with the dealers of the true **Nam** —*
> *And, thus, accumulate the wealth of truth."*

Become a Dealer in Horses

Not to be disheartened, the father tried another ploy. "Why don't you think of becoming a dealer in horses?"

But Nanak had words of wisdom for the ancient trade too. Sang he:

"A true dealer of horses should breed horses of truth,
Store the wealth of virtue to meet the needs of the way
And worry no more.
For, full of unfailing faith in the abode of the Formless,
He shall share its bliss."

Then why not take up a Job?

Even though rebuffed each time in this manner, Mehta Kalu still persisted. He said if nothing else appealed to him then why not think of joining a government job?

But pat came another hymn, rejecting the suggestion.

"I serve my Master whom you too should serve
With all your heart.
*Perform actions with His **Nam** written in your heart.*
Your face shall shine with fourfold splendour
And you shall be greatly blessed."

An Honest and Truthful Bargain

One day Mehta Kalu came up with a proposal which Nanak could not refuse. He asked Nanak: "Son, would you learn how to make honest and truthful bargains that are

Nanak feeding the hungry *Sadhu*s in the belief that it blesses the giver, both in this world, and the world hereafter.

6

also profitable at the same time?" To this Nanak readily said yes. Next day, Mehta Kalu gave him twenty rupees in hard cash and said, " Son! Go to the market, purchase something cheaper and sell it at a higher price. This is the way of making a truthful and profitable bargain." Kalu also sent Bala Sandhu, a childhood pal of Nanak in attendance, lest he faltered somewhere.

On the way, Nanak met a group of ascetics, sitting in a deserted grove. He went to them and asked, "Why are you sitting here?"

They answered, "We remain away from big places as they are evil. And, besides our needs are so few that we depend upon God who provides for everyone He creates."

Nanak asked, "Noble Sirs, when did you eat a full meal last?"

The answer was, "Five days ago." However, what intrigued Nanak was that they had no idea of a full meal. Moved, Nanak offered them the money he had. But the ascetics said that they would not touch it as it was the root of all evil. Then Nanak and Bala went to the market and purchased many provisions and eatables. On the way back, Nanak gave the ascetics everything.

Now, they started for home. When they neared their village, Nanak sent Bala ahead to narate the incident to his father. When his father heard the story, he beat his chest and pulled his hair. He, along with Rai Bular, asked Nanak for an explanation.

Nanak explained that his father wanted him to make an honest and profitable bargain, and he could not think of a more honest and profitable bargain than this as it would bless the giver both here and hereafter.

This reply was not unexpected for Rai Bular. He turned to Kalu and said, "Listen! Your son is not meant for the gains of this world. His gains are the gains of heaven."

Nanak's Mother

At home, Nanak's mother was relieved that her son was back with her. However she said, "Son, I do not understand what you mean by the True *Nam* . . ."

At that Nanak burst forth singing:

> *"To remember Him is to live*
> *To forget Him is to die.*
> *It is difficult to expound the True* **Nam**
>
> *"When hunger for it awakens in the heart*
> *All other hungers depart.*
> *And it consumes all suffering".*

The mother said, "They say only the great Pandits can know Him. Can a poor woman like me have such fortune?"

Nanak smiled,

> *"They alone are of low birth*
> *Who forget the true Master.*
> *Without the grace of His **Nam***
> *Everyone's status is low."*

Arrival of a dear Sister

When Kalu had lost all hope of making Nanak a man of the world, Nanaki, his sister came to them along with her husband Jai Ram, like a divine messenger.

Her proposal was that her husband would find Nanak a job at Kartarpur and when he was somewhat settled, she would find a suitable girl for him to marry. This would change Nanak completely. This was a time-tested formula of reforming such wayward youngmen. It was tried on the young Siddharth as well, who later became the Buddha.

Happily, Nanak too consented to his going to Sultanpur to be able to live with his sister. It was a very eventful change in his life.

First Stage of the Mission

Nanak was about 17 when he came to live at Sultanpur. Soon, Jai Ram got him the job of a storekeeper in the service of Nawab Daulat Khan Lodhi. His precise position was that of a *'Modi'*. The job though a lowly one, was yet responsible. The State revenues were then collected in kind and stored in granaries. The State payments were also made in kind and from the same granaries.

This meant that all surpluses and shortfalls of the stored grain had to be accounted for in the books by none other than the storekeeper himself. In the course of his duties, Nanak had to physically weigh all that was received as well as all that was given out and keep the record accurate. Thus, those who knew Nanak to be a wayward person were astonished at the diligence and competence with which he discharged his laborious duties.

It was at Sultanpur that Nanak married Sulakhani and had from her two sons who too, in due time, became famous as great ascetics. Nanak lived in Sultanpur for nearly 15 years — a period highly important in terms of his evolution from Nanak Dev to Guru Nanak.

The job that Nanak held excited jealousy among others. People made all kinds of complaints against him. One of the repeated complaints was that Nanak's work area was the meeting place of all beggars, castaways and anchorites of the town and near about. It was also rumoured that Nanak munificently looked after the needs of these good-for-nothings.

Another very interesting thing was that whenever Nanak reached the number 13 while weighing, he would repeat this number endlessly. 13 or *'terah'* in the local language, means "I am yours" and like a person drunk on the wine of the **Nam**, he could not proceed any further even though he would continue to weigh accurately. This strange habit enraged some people who went straight to the Nawab.

Ultimately, the Nawab ordered a thorough inquiry of the stores held by Nanak. When Nanak was finally vindicated, the records showed that Nanak had to be paid something in lieu of the settlement. Soon after, Nanak decided to leave the job.

Hence, Jai Ram duly admonished him but Nanak said, "My account with the Nawab is closed. Now a new chapter of my mission is going to start."

"And what's that mission?" asked Jai Ram.

Nanak weighing the grain at the Modikhana of the Nawab, as the official storekeeper. It was here that he would always get stuck at the number thirteen or *'Terah'* which means "I am yours, O Lord!".

"To bring men closer to God so that they enjoy treasures of happiness."

"Where are the treasures of happiness in this world of woe?" inquired Jai Ram.

"They are within you," Nanak replied. Jai Ram voiced his concern over what appeared to be Nanak's renunciation of the world. But Nanak said, "Haven't I married? Haven't I sired children? Haven't I fulfilled all my worldly duties? So, none need worry about me on that account."

Worldly Snares Rejected

When the Guru finally decided to leave his small world at Sultanpur to devote himself to removing spiritual darkness from the world at large, a thousand and one worldly snares started dancing before his eyes. *Kaliyuga* (the age of evil) trembled and was concerned that if the enlightenment of **Nam** grew, it could not establish the Satan's rule in the world. At first the *Kaliyuga* frightened Nanak endlessly. And when the Guru remained firm in his resolve, it heaped many an allurement before him; palaces and pleasure groves flowing with milk and honey. Not just that, countless maidens of unsurpassed beauty paraded before his mind's eye to make him desist from his chosen path. But the Guru just smiled and said:

"Pearl-built peerless palaces,
Adorned with precious gems,
Fragrant with all the scents of earth —
*These delude fools who forget His **Nam**."*

He also brushed aside all the riches that the earth treasures in its belly. Viewing their regal parade, he merely smiled and said:

"Were the earth blazing with diamonds,
And sparkling with rubies,
Or, overflowing with maidens of glamorous beauty —
These delude only the fools."

Then the supernatural powers offered themselves to be at the service of the Guru. But he rejected them with the same disdain, saying:

"If I exercise supernatural powers
And can create wealth at a gesture.
Or, appear and disappear at will
And thus win popular acclaim —
These delude only the fools."

In short, the Guru discarded with scorn all that the heaven and the earth could heap before him and his mind remained calm like a placid lake.

In the Presence of God

Nanak was in this God-intoxicated mood when something extraordinary happened. The event that took place is truly stranger than fiction. The story goes thus: One fine morning, Nanak had gone to the river Bein for his usual ablutions, and as he took a dip in the river, he suddenly disappeared in the waves. His clothes were lying at a particular spot on the bank but Nanak was nowhere to be found. The river was thoroughly searched but in vain. There was no proof that Nanak had not drowned. Nor was there any evidence to believe that he was still alive.

But, 72 hours later, Nanak reappeared at the same spot where he had taken his plunge into the river. And as soon as he came out, the first sentence he uttered to the gathered concourse of Hindus and Muslims, was *"Na koi Hindu; na Mussalman."* (There is neither a Hindu nor a Mussalman).

The news of Nanak's reappearance in this manner had made Nanak a man of God. He was no longer the Nanak that people had known. So, what he spoke to them came to be known as the Sermon of Sultanpur, prefaced as it was by the *Mool Mantra* or the basic surd of Sikhism.

Here Nanak as Guru Nanak is seen collaring the *Kaliyuga* that personifies the age of sin and darkness, as the *Kaliyuga* cannot stay where righteousness prevails.

11

However, the story that spread was that as soon as Nanak took a dip into the river, the divine messengers took him to God's presence. The *Mool Mantra* with which opens the *Japuji* and the Guru Granth is the prayer Nanak spontaneously sang in praise of God. Thereupon, God commanded Nanak to go back to the world to save the suffering humanity. Not just that, He made him sip from a bowl the nectar of the **Nam** and ordained him as '*Guru Parmeshwar*', He Himself remaining the '*Par Brahm Parmeshwar*'. Thus, Nanak became the designated Guru of God's own chosen path.

The 'Sermon at Sultanpur' over time came to be known as the *Japuji*, the first prayer of the Sikhs. It is believed that Nanak spent the better part of those three days at the '*Sach Khand*', the highest region of God's domain where eternal bliss alone reigns. Both the *Mool Mantra* and the *Japuji* are, Nanak's redefinition of God and the basis of his own spiritual agenda.

Normally only the most credulous would believe such a story. But the fact that this episode had changed Nanak completely leaves no scope for us to doubt its veracity. In the course of those three days, he had changed from Nanak Dev to Guru Nanak, the world teacher. Now he had become simply irresistible — a storehouse of divine wisdom and a profoundly magnetic personality.

Nanak, on emerging from the river Bein, proclaiming forthwith his universal message: 'There's No Hindu, no Mussalman' in God's own scheme of things. This is the crux of what we know as his 'Sermon of Sultanpur'.

Summoned to the Court

By uttering the words *"Na koi Hindu; na Mussalman,"* Nanak had committed the ultimate blasphemy in terms of the reigning bigotry of the age. Since those were the times of extreme religious intolerance, it was not possible to decry the spiritual superiority of the Muslims and get away with it. And Nanak had done just that by equating the Muslims and the Hindus.

Hence, Nanak was summoned to the Court without delay. However, when the first summons came, Nanak refused to comply with them, saying that he was no longer in the Nawab's service. Then, the Qazi himself came to fetch him.

When Nanak finally made his appearance in court, the Nawab was all consideration for him and made him sit close to him. Then he said, "What puzzles me is your statement that 'there's no Hindu; there's no Mussalman.' Will you kindly explain as to what you mean by it?"

In reply Nanak said, "To serve Him, there's no Hindu; there's no Muslim. All are equal in His court. Still, God wishes every Hindu to be a good Hindu just as he wants every Mussalman to be a good Mussalman."

"Nanak, who in your opinion is a good Muslim? Is the Qazi a good Muslim or not?"

Upon that, Nanak started to sing his description of a true Muslim. This description is as follows:

> *"He who is firm in his faith*
> *Has a right to be called a Muslim.*
> *His acts must accord with the faith of the Prophet;*
> *He must clean his heart of pride and greed,*
> *No more troubled by the two imposters — life and death.*
>
> *"Resigned to the will of God,*
> *Knowing Him as the Doer,*
> *Freed from domination of the self,*
> *Compassionate to all things —*
> *Such a one may call himself a Muslim."*

Now the wily Qazi tried to corner Nanak in a different way. He asked him if he was a Hindu or a Muslim.

Nanak replied, "I am neither a Hindu nor a Muslim."

"How come?" the Nawab asked.

Nanak said, "Only the one who lives in the light of God's word as brought down to the earth by prophets of all religions can call himself a truly religious man. To me, all religions are His and hence equally sacred."

It was difficult for the Nawab to accept such an equality. How could Hinduism be as sacred as Islam? He, therefore, asked Nanak that if all religions were equally sacred, then would he mind offering the *Namaz* with them?

Nanak walking out victorious from his first trial at the Court of Nawab Daulat Khan Lodhi, to take up his mission of serving the deluded and suffering humanity.

"With pleasure," said Nanak. So, he was made to stand between the Nawab and the Qazi. But when the congregation kneeled, Nanak did not. At that the Qazi thundered, "You must know you have committed a serious blasphemy. Now what have you to say to it?"

Nanak was unhustled. He asked the Qazi, "Tell me Sir, whether the *Namaz* is merely kneeling and bowing?"

"No, not. These are merely the outward expressions of it. For, the essence of the *Namaz* is the words of the prayer."

At that said Nanak, "If that is so then neither the Nawab nor your goodself was offering the *Namaz*. While you were thinking of the foal just born to your mare, the Nawab Sahib's mind was roaming somewhere in Qandhar with his agents, who were sent to purchase horses."

And so came to Nanak his first victory of the divine mission he was about to launch.

14

Preparing For His Odysseys or Long *Udasis*

Between Nanak's emergence from the river and his court encounter, he had spent some time in the local cremation ground. It is here that he had drawn up the critical parts of his divine agenda to be followed during his long *Udasis*.

Most men and women who came to see him however thought that some evil spirit had taken possession of him. At this, Jai Ram was deeply distressed. He consulted a Moulvi who was known to be an expert exorcist. When he sat before him, the Guru addressed him thus:

> *"He whose heart is filled with the love of the Lord,*
> *And who considers himself less than the dust . . .*
> *And all else superior to him, can such a one lack sanity?"*

The Moulvi immediately got the message and turning to Jai Ram said "There is nothing wrong with the young man."

It is here that his sister and wife came to meet him. They wanted Nanak to let them know why he was leaving them for his *Udasis*. But his mind was made up and he told them, "The entire humanity is now my family. In serving humanity I serve you too."

During this time having earned God's grace, he had become a celestial poet and transcendental singer. Armed with the powers of the **Nam,** he could not now be

Nanak, in the dress he evolved for himself that suited his mission. It was neither of the Hindus nor of the Muslims.

15

worsted in argument and debate and even in spiritual attainment. Thus, equipped with the most effective tools of communication, he decided to set out on his long *Udasi*s (tours) that took him to all the four corners of the then known world of Hinduism and Islam.

But it was a long and arduous task to persuade people to take to his path of godliness by meeting and conquering most of the known spiritual and divine leaders of both religions. For, that way alone, he could help people separate chaff from the grain. And the common mass of people never let him down. They just lauded and applauded him wherever he went.

So, with this end in view, he summoned from his birthplace his childhood pals, Bala Sandhu, a Hindu Jat and Mardana, a Muslim rebec player. And accompanied by them, he launched upon his *Udasi*s or Odyssey to the known world of religion. His simple mission was now to remove the darkness that enveloped the fugitive souls everywhere, ushering them into light of faith and hope. He spent 20 long years of his life on these *Udasi*s.

He also evolved a dress for himself that uniquely suited his mission. It was neither of the Hindus nor of the Muslims. The old *Janam Sakhi* records it thus, "Nanak now wore a strange motley; a mango-coloured jacket over which he threw a white sheet, a hat like that of a Muslim anchorite, with a necklace of bones around his neck, and a frontal mark of saffron, imprinted on the forehead in the style of a Hindu devotee." In fact, none could even identify if he was a *Sanyasi* or a householder.

Nanak's *Udasi*s or His World Conquest   Chapter III

Before we attempt a brief account of these spiritual tours or *Udasi*s of Nanak, we need to mention that we do not mean to present them in their chronological or geographical order. Rather, we have grouped them subject-wise under five heads viz. (1) Social Protest; (2) Encounter with the *Siddha*s; (3) Encounter with the Muslim Divines; (4) Cleansing the Muck of Falsehood from the Hindu Sacred Places; and (5) Visiting the Lake Mansarovar with a Lama. A brief account of these *Udasi*s is as under:

Social Protest

In effect, his first and last *Udasi* both of whom took place in Saidpur or Eminabad, are great events of social protest. The first took place in or about 1501-2 AD when Nanak was around 32 years of age and the last in 1521 AD when he was about 52 years of age, which means a distance of at least 20 years stood between them. The rest of his *Udasi*s fall in-between.

Saidpur or Eminabad was important in the life of Guru Nanak in that his first-ever disciple or Sikh, Bhai Lalo lived there. That's why, Lalo prominently figures in both the

With Bhai Lalo, the carpenter, who became the first disciple or Sikh of Guru Nanak.

Guru Nanak demonstrating how the hard-earned bread of Lalo, even if bland and coarse, is full of nectar while the rich man's *Parathas*, soaked with milk and ghee, are full of the blood of the exploited.

events. Let's know more about these two events of Nanak's unique social protest:

Food that's Nectar

It so happened that when the Guru came to Saidpur from Sultanpur and was staying with Bhai Lalo, Malik Bhago, the Hindu grandee of the place was observing the *Shraddha* ceremony (obsequy feast) of his late father. So, along with all the *Brahmin*s of the town, he also invited all men of God in or about the town to partake of that feast and bless his dead father's soul. But Nanak did not turn up. He preferred to break bread with the lowly carpenter. He was asked to explain the reason why he insulted Malik Bhago.

Without skirting the issue even for a minute, Nanak procured Bhago's rich *parathas* and the hard bread of Lalo. Then, holding them in his two hands, he squeezed them. While blood of the exploited flowed from Malik's *Parathas*, a stream of life-giving nectar trickled from the dried bread. Nanak made his point of 'unjust' income.

Encounter with Babur

When Nanak during his return journey from Baghdad in 1520-21 AD passed through Kabul, Babur was preparing for his third invasion of India. His second invasion of India had been frustrated by the resistance that the Faujdar of Saidpur had offered. Hence, this town was the main target of his ferocity. Nanak came there just before Babur and hence was a witness to its sack. The heart-rending story of this sack is the subject-matter of Nanak's Babur *Bani* that forms such a conspicuous part of Sri Guru Granth Sahib. It is a unique piece of poetry in the religious literature of the world in that men of God are not normally expected to react to victors or powers as Nanak did. Since this *Bani* is addressed to Lalo, it is both graphic and authentic.

He prefaces his *Bani* with these words, "What descends from the God above and as it descends from Him, so I speak it, O Lalo!" A few excerpts from the Babur *Bani* are as under:

"O Lalo! Babur has hastened from Kabul
With a bridal procession of sin
And demands wealth as his bride.
The call of duty and religion are forgotten.
Falsehood marches in the van, O Lalo!
Qazis *and* Brahmins *are no more called,*
The devil reads the marriage vows, O Lalo!"

Further says Nanak:

"I hear the paeans of murder
And see men smeared with the saffron of blood.
Sing praises of the Lord in the city of corpses
And dwell on the truth:
He who made men, assigned them different positions,
And sits apart alone and regards them.
True is the Lord and true His disposition;
True is the justice He metes out."

The suffering of civil population so moved Nanak that he did not spare even God's indifference to it. Complaining to God, said he:

"You are the Lord Creator of all beings;
I wouldn't mind if a strong person were to beat another
  strong person,
But when a powerful lion pounces upon a hapless herd
  of cows,
Is it not the master who is to answer for such an
  injustice?"

And as to the reigning Lodhi masters, he castigated them most ruthlessly. Said he:

"The jewel of Hindustan has been thrown away by the
  dogs (Lodhis)

When they are dead and gone, none will remember them."

Guru Nanak denouncing Babur for his inhuman sack of Eminabad, describing it as the 'city of corpses'.   19

As about the priests who bragged about their miraculous powers of *Jantar Mantar*, Nanak lampooned them thus:

"He (Babur) burnt houses, mansions and palaces.
He cut princes to pieces and rolled them in the dust.
No Moghul has become blind;
No priest has wrought a miracle."

Not that such an outspoken denunciation went unnoticed. The local legend has it that Babur's men arrested Nanak. Like the others jailed, he too was condemned to move a millstone to grind the grain. However, soon Babur realized that he had put behind bar a true man of God and so he was released. But even so, Nanak emerges as the first conscientious *Satyagrahi* of India.

Encounters with the *Siddha*s

In Nanak's time, the *Siddha Jogi*s dominated the spiritual scene of Punjab with their supernatural miracles, weird mutterings and against-the-nature *siddhi*s (attainments), thus beguiling the youngmen to turn away from the life of a householder. Nanak had several encounters with them, the reason being that unless he was able to thoroughly debunk them, he could not have made householders as the focal point of all godly pursuits — Nanak's basic premise that distinguishes Sikhism from other spiritual paths and religions of the world.

Guru Nanak blessing Babur when the latter came to beg pardon from him for his indiscretion in arresting him in the first instance.

Another reason for his encounter with the *Siddha*s was that looking at the noble visage of Nanak as well as his spiritual achievements, various groups of the *Siddha*s wanted to enlist him as a member of their group. In their estimation, it could have meant a great accession to their own prestige.

The *Siddha*s, which means the Nath *Jogi*s in the main, was an old cult and such was their prestige that even some Muslims had become their followers. For, most people believed that they could fly in the air, walk on water and disappear at will or become smaller than an ant or bigger than an elephant and could even live longer than ordinary beings. However, Nanak knew better.

But, people at large were mighty afraid of the 'Siddhas' even though some of them practised all kinds of corruptions including taking intoxicants and indulging in sexual orgies. A particular branch of these *Jogi*s even used women as a means of salvation. Hence, in the name of true God and religion, Nanak was determined to expose them.

Nanak believed that it did not require of one to renounce one's home to become spiritual. The *Jogi*s naturally disapproved of his preachings of achieving spiritual knowledge and insight by living in the real world.

Nanak faced one persistent inquiry from the *Jogi*s and that was to identify his denomination. To which Guru did Nanak belong?

To the last question Nanak's pertinent reply was, "I belong to the denomination of God." This means God Himself was his Guru. Now, let us see how Nanak elaborated upon it. Sang he:

> *"In every heart He dwells.*
> *Dedicate your will to His service.*
> *Coming and departing is the Law.*
> *Accept the divine will.*
> *The true teacher imparts the secret*
> *Of finding an abiding place in God.*
> *They who know the word of the Guru*
> *Realize the self and become one with Him."*

At another place, he told the *Siddha*s the meaning of emancipation — the ultimate spiritual quest — and how to attain it. He said:

> *"He is hidden in every heart.*
> *He whom the Guru instructs is emancipated.*
> *The uninstructed is born and dies.*
> *The aspirant through the alchemy of the* **Nam**
> *Becomes one with the True One.*
> *Swallowed by illusion and bound by ignorance,*
> *The unawakened is lost.*
> *By the Guru's instructions is He found,*
> *Darkness is dispelled, egoism is destroyed,*
> *And the aspirant becomes one with God."*

Guru Nanak admonishing the *Siddha Jogi*s in their haunts in the inner Himalayas for having left the world of commitment.

Thus, the *Jogi*s were always perplexed by Nanak's down-to-earth logic and such simple, homely truths. Sometimes they would resort to technical questions about Yoga. Being quite adept in the vocabulary of Yoga, he was always ready with answers.

In all the dialogues, the most important point that generally emerged was that Nanak was able to impress upon the *Jogi*s the futility of their hard-earned *siddhi*s and the superiority of his own *Sehaj* or effortless path of the **Nam**. For, that could enable one to control the five passions, rise above desires and surrender the self to the divine will. And the householders were somehow better fitted to do this than the professional adepts. In fact, this concept of gradual but sure transcendence through the alchemy of the **Nam** always turned out to be a sure winner for Nanak.

Nanak lost no opportunity of bearding them in their own dens as it were. For example, not only did he go to the inner Himalayas, he also visited them in Gorakh Hatti near Peshawar, in Almora and Pilibhit, at their fair in Achal Batala and even in the Jungles of Assam.

A Nanak Miracle

Nanak even beat them at their own game of performing miracles. Let us see here just one miracle that he is known to have performed while being tested by Bhartari, the *Siddha*, in his hermitage in Assam.

This particular *Jogi* was known to be very old, indeed ancient, having almost conquered death and become immortal. When they came face to face with each other, said Bhartari to Nanak, "Listen, O boy! I inherit the wisdom of centuries. Our system has endured from the beginning of time. Its truths have never been challenged. So, you should accept my invitation and join me as a disciple."

But Nanak, in all humility, said, "Age is no evidence of the real merit of any system. Besides, there is no evidence that your system has ever been able to conquer the five basic evils, viz. passion, anger, greed, attachment and I-amness."

"Have you any real power beyond your glib tongue?" asked Bhartari badly offended.

Nanak, at the *Siddha* Bhartari's hermitage in Assam performing his miracle when he was put to test.

23

"None, " said the Guru, "I do nothing against the laws of God. He alone can perform miracles."

Ridiculing Nanak, said Bhartari, "You see this disciple of mine, sitting before me. Just watch him. He will rise to the skies and become invisible in no time. Now if you have any power, then bring him back to the earth." And wonder of wonders! The disciple flew upwards and became invisible.

Then Bhartari with utter disdain said to Nanak, "Try to catch him if you can."

Nanak remained unprovoked. But in his characteristic way, he only smiled. And as soon as he did, his sandals flew up in the sky. After a short while what they saw was that the disciple was descending and the pair of sandals were beating him. The disciple fell at the feet of Guru Nanak.

But the 'miracle-saga' did not stop there. All of a sudden, Guru Nanak disappeared. Seeing this happen, Bhartari went in search of him. After a long time, the *Jogi* returned and confessed his inability to find the Guru. But he had hardly said so when they found the Guru seated in his former place amongst them.

The *Siddha*s were simply overwhelmed with awe and wonder. Thus were they fully vanquished.

Encounters with the Muslim Divines

In Nanak's time, the Muslim Sufis and divines were deeply immersed in the environment of Punjab. They had adopted a monastic life-style of divine love and mysticism and set up their *khanakah*s (monasteries) at various places in Punjab. They were popular both with the Hindus and the Muslims. However, they were different from the *Qazi*s and *Mullah*s of the official Muslim orthodoxy.

In short, in the people's eye they were much known and respected for their spiritual attainments and piety. Kings and commoners alike were their followers.

In a way, Islam was reaching out to the Hindu masses mainly through their devotional idiom and good offices. Some of them were also instruments of converting the Hindus to Islam but mainly through love and persuasion. Music and poetry and the use of folk idiom were their main tools. It is also apparent that Nanak held many of them in great reverence. Hence, he made a special point to visit as many of them as possible. In particular, he visited the Sufi masters in Pak Pattan, Multan, Mian Mithe ka Kotla, Panipat, etc. before going to Mecca and Baghdad. Here we shall take note of only four of his encounters.

(a)   Being a great fan of Sheikh Farid, Nanak first visited his monastery at Pak Pattan. At that time, Sheikh Behram was the head of the monastery. Sitting on the outskirts of the town, Nanak began to sing a composition, rich in Sufi texture. Its words were:

> *"You yourself are the writing tablet;*
> *You are the pen and you are the writer;*
> *You are also the written word;*
> *You are the one without a second."*

When the Sheikh came to know of it, he wanted to find out the singer's credentials before he could come to meet him. He therefore sent a disciple to ask the Guru: "There is but one God. However, there are two ways: Which should one accept and which one to reject?" Nanak instantly replied, "There is only one God and there is only one way. Stick to that way alone."

This reply so pleased the Sheikh that he came out to meet the Guru. He said, "The Hindus deny the God of Islam. Likewise, the Muslims accuse the Hindus of worshipping many gods. Yet, you say 'there is only one God as also only one way to reach Him.' How come?"

Now the Guru replied to it in another hymn of his. The words are:

> *"God is one;*
> *He is not subject to change;*
> *His light is the life of creation.*
> *That which is born and dies*
> *Cannot be the subject of worship."*

It now enabled them to exchange many of their thoughts in the typical Sufi format. At the end of a profound dialogue, the Sheikh asked, "It is easy to speak of God but difficult to kindle the heart with devotion. So, how should one proceed?"

The Guru in reply sang a '*shabad*' of none other than Sheikh Farid himself:

> *"They indeed are true-hearted*
> *In whose heart dwells nothing but the love of God.*
> *They who have one thing in their heart*
> *And another on the lips*
> *Are immature and unripe …*
> *They are truly imbued with the divine*
> *Who stand straight in His sight,*
> *Like beggars at His gate,*
> *With love of the Lord in their hearts.*
> *Blessed is the mother who begot them;*
> *Blessed is the earth of which they are the ripe fruit."*

The Sheikh and the Guru formed an enduring friendship. The Guru stayed with the Sheikh for some more days and discoursed to thousands of his disciples. The Guru visited him once more but this time to collect the *shloka*s of Shaikh Farid that were later included in the Guru Granth. The Sheikh too came to see the Guru at Kartarpiur but at the very fag end of his life.

Guru Nanak placing a Jasmine petal in the bowl of milk to assure the *Pir* of his unthreathening presence in the monastery.

(b)   The second most important encounter of the Guru was at Multan — at that time known as the home of Sufis. The city was the seat of a legendary Sufi named Pir Baha-ud-Din whose followers were truly legion. When the Guru reached there, the Pir-in-charge of the monastery sent him a bowl of milk so full that not a drop more could be added to it. At that, the Guru placed a jasmine petal on it and returned the bowl. It was a subtle exchange of messages. The Pir had meant that the place was so full of godmen that there was no place for any more. In reply, the Guru had meant that he would remain in the town as unobtrusively as the jasmine petal floats in the bowl of milk.

On receiving the message, the Pir joined Guru Nanak who received him with great warmth.

The Pir then asked Nanak, "Tell me how the world came into existence . . ."

The Guru answered, "To know the reality, the first pre-requisite is that any sense of separateness from the reality must disappear. Else, it is difficult to find out the why and wherefore of existence."

Instantly overwhelmed by emotion, the Pir kissed the Guru's hand. It transported him into ecstasy as Nanak began to sing:

> "Come brother! Let's embrace each other
> For, now we belong to One.
> Now that we have come together
> We shall talk only of our Beloved, our Lord.
> His are all virtues; all evils are in us."

26

The Pir then sent away his disciples and decided to judge Nanak's wisdom personally. He asked Nanak the subtlest question about his credo. He said, "Pray, tell me what power is inherent in the *Nam* as you call it."

The Guru was happy to say, "The Word is the first manifestation of the Unmanifest. From it flows the entire universe. It has the power to draw into itself whatever flows from it in the first instance. The *Nam* is the only representation of the Creator in the universe. It can be uttered in all its power after complete purification of the mind and heart is obtained."

The Pir asked, "Can you prove the power of the word to reabsorb and recreate?"

The Guru merely smiled and said, "Calm yourself; wait a minute."

Then he put his hand on the head of the Pir and uttered the Divine Word. The Pir was reduced to ashes that very instant. The Guru once again uttered the Divine Word, looking at the ashes and the Pir reappeared, sitting in his own place. The Pir fell on the feet of the Guru and begged him to teach him how to achieve salvation.

The Guru sung:

> *"It would be right to make a permanent place*
> *And escape the pain of daily wanderings*
> *If there were a permanent place anywhere*
> *And the world were unchanging."*

(c)   The Guru now proceeded to Mecca, holiest of the holy centres of pilgrimage in Islam. This visit of the Guru is the most well-known event of his life. The story goes thus:

On reaching Mecca, Nanak was greatly tired and so he fell asleep with his feet towards the holy Kaaba. Now this was a cardinal sacrilege in the eyes of the devout, particularly when the prayer time was at hand. The priest who saw Nanak in that position was greatly enraged. Shouting at the Guru, he said, "Wake up you stupid fool and rub your nose (in contrition) on the ground for sleeping with your feet in the direction of the house of God." Half-asleep, Nanak merely said, "I am too tired to move. Please turn my feet in the direction in which God does not dwell."

This insolence further enraged the priest. He asked the keeper of the Kaaba to catch hold of the stranger by his feet and give them a right about-turn. But whichever direction he turned the Guru's feet, the Kaaba turned too. The point the Guru wanted to make was that there was not a place in space where God did not dwell. The priest understood that the stranger was no ordinary mortal.

The miracle was duly reported to the chief priest of the Kaaba, Maulvi Rukun-ud-Din. As a genuine seeker of

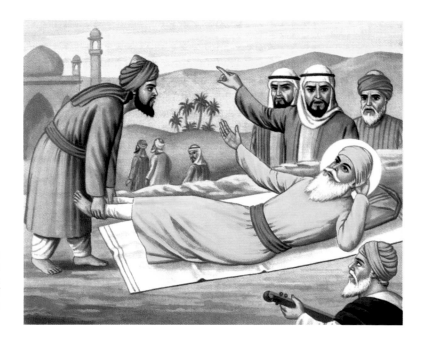

Guru Nanak at Mecca sleeping with his feet towards the Kaaba, the home of Allah. Here, the keeper of the Kaaba is seen trying to turn the feet of the Guru in a direction where Allah is not present.

the truth, he rushed to where the Guru was sleeping and then addressed him:

"You are, to all appearances, a godly man. Will you kindly tell me which religion do you belong to?"

"I belong to the religion of the One who is the master of all that's visible and invisible."

"What do you exactly mean by the One you have in mind?" asked Rukun-ud-Din.

"He who is without a second. To whom neither the birth nor the death is known. Who is beyond all change and who pervades everywhere — lands, seas and skies."

"That means you believe in one God. So, you must be a Muslim," said the *Maulvi*.

"I accept no creed. I am His slave, and slaves as a rule, have no will of their own." said the Guru, "How can the one who owes unwavering allegiance to the Lord accept a creed other than His?"

"God as you have described Him is the same as our *Kalima* speaks. Then why not acknowledge that you are a Muslim?" asked Rukun-ud-Din.

"The *Veda*s too speak of one God, the supreme Self. Then why should I not declare myself a Hindu. Truth remains truth; it is the lenses of the self that reflect it in various colours. A servant of God, aware of His presence, cannot accept creeds that imprison the truth," said Nanak.

"How do you say so?" asked Rukun-ud-Din.

"You have an example before you. You call this sacred temple a house of God. But if you are a true believer then you find that there is no place anywhere where the house of God is not. Besides, when you say that you are a believer in one God, then why don't you recognize the fact that men of diverse creeds are your brothers only?"

This finally rendered the high priest speechless.

(d) At Hasan Abdal, alternatively known as Panja Sahib, now in Pakistan, lived Wali Qandhari, a Muslim divine of considerable supernatural powers. He lived mostly alone and in meditation. During his *Udasis*, the Guru with Mardana in attendance also came there and stopped at the foot of the hillock on which lived the Wali.

They had come there after a very tiring journey and Mardana was feeling very thirsty. But there was no water around. The only well at the top of the hillock was for the personal use of the Wali. So, at the bidding of the Guru, Mardana went up and bowing to the Wali, said, "I am the servant of Nanak, a holy man. I am feeling thirsty. My Guru has sent me here to be able to drink water from the well."

The Wali took it as an offence that Nanak had personally not paid obeisance to him. So, with anger in his heart, he said, "You cannot drink water from here. If your Nanak is indeed a holy man, then how come he could not procure water for you?"

When Mardana, reported all this to the Guru, he sent him back to the Wali and asked him to be very humble while asking for water. But he again received the same kind of rebuff. This time the words were, "Ask your Guru to produce water if he can. You cannot drink water from my well."

When Mardana returned he was really very thirsty. Then the Guru said, "Mardana, dig a little hole where you are sitting. God willing, water will flow."

Mardana did as commanded and the miracle did happen. For, the little hole started to flow with water. A strange thing happened simultaneously. The well of the Wali began

Guru Nanak at Hasan Abdal in Punjab stretching his arm to stop the heavy stone pushed in his direction by the angered Wali Qandhari.

Guru Nanak at Baghdad addressing
the Muslim divines and noblemen –
one of the rare panels at the
Golden Temple.

30

to empty. On comprehending it, the Wali's rage knew no bounds. So, to kill Nanak, he hurled a big stone downhill.

But the Guru did not move away from the falling stone. He just raised his hand in a gesture for the stone to stop, and it stopped as soon as it touched Nanak's hand. (The stone and the pond are testimony to the story even today. The stone also carries the imprint of the Nanak's hand.)

This frightened the Wali no end. So, in an instant, he came down to pay his respects to the Guru. And after Nanak received him with affection and made him sit beside him, the Wali asked, "How did you acquire this power?"

The Guru's answer was casual. He said, "I have no power. All power belongs to God. It is only when we take shelter in Him that He showers His powers on us."

Sweeping the Impurities of Falsehood from the Hindu Sacred Places

Likewise, the Guru went round almost all the well-known Hindu pilgrim spots in India such as Kurukshetra, Hardwar, Prayag, Benaras, Gaya, Jagannath Puri, Kanchi, Rameshwaram, Singhal Dweep or modern Sri Lanka, Kanya Kumari, Kerala, Srirangapatnam, Mathura, Pushkar, Ujjain, Nasik, etc. The Guru always tried to reach these places when there were sufficient number of pilgrims. He pertinently made a point to debunk the priests and how they misled and fleeced the gullible.

However, at almost all these places the most curious thing that happened was that he found most pilgrims quite eager and ready to listen to him. Perhaps the time was just ripe when someone like him attacked the empty ritual and exposed its high priests. He also set up the *sangat*s (congregation) of his disciples at the places he visited. That's how, while attacking hypocrisy and falsehood, he also established *sangat*s (societies of holy men) of his new religion. We propose to visit along with him only about half a dozen of these places to see their formation.

At Kurukshetra

Kurukshetra was the first stop in his pilgrimage to the Hindu sacred places. There was a solar eclipse on the day of his arrival. Thousands upon thousands of devout Hindus had come to take a dip in the holy tanks, make charities and pray for the release of the sun-god from the clutches of the demon Rahu. The Guru thought it to be the right time to draw the attention of the erring humanity from the unreal to the real; from external ritual ceremonies to the inner truth.

Nanak was sitting near the Brahm Sar, one of the most sacred Kurukshetra tanks when a prince gave him a piece

Guru Nanak accepting deer's meat offered to him by a prince at the holy site of Kurukshetra.

of deer's flesh, that he had hunted just in the vicinity of Kurukshetra only a short while ago. The Guru asked Bala, his Hindu companion to cook it. Bala obeyed. But cooking a deer at Kurukshetra and that too on a solar-eclipse day was too big a sacrilege to be condoned. Hence, it caused great consternation. A very large and threatening crowd gathered there, almost ready to stone the Guru. The Brahmin priests were duly instigating it.

But just when the things seemed to go out of hand, the Guru stood up and spoke to the crowd and his words acted as a soothing balm of utmost potency. In an instant the people got ready to listen to him. In a nutshell, he told the crowd that those who harbour evil thoughts in their hearts and under the cloak of abstinence aspire to holy living know not the truth. Then he sang the following hymn of his:

> "Fools wrangle about eating meat.
> They know not the truth, or the way of right action,
> Or the difference between meat and vegetables,
> The acts that are sinful and those that are not."
> . . . .
> "They, the man-eaters, pitiless and cruel,
> Hold their noses and forswear flesh —
> Is it any good telling the blind
> Who cannot see or act upon what is right?"

"So you call those who disagree with you blind men!" exclaimed a *Brahmin* priest with deep resentment.

"They are indeed blind who act blindly," said the Guru, "Whose hearts are unawakened; they who would see their parents starve and do nothing to relieve them of their suffering but raise their voices in holy horror if anyone ate the meat."

Continuing he said, "Man is born in flesh, nursed in flesh and is a tabernacle of flesh. Men call themselves Pandits without knowledge and without doing what is right. For them, eating meat is sinful but gratifying greed is not. All living things are made of flesh."

The words of the Guru in some strange way seemed to possess the mind of the crowd. They felt something they had never felt before as they felt drawn toward the truth. In the end, the Guru said, "You care for the shell and disregard the spirit. For you, the untruth has become the truth."

Those who had come to stone the Guru, readily opted to become his disciples and built a *Dharmasal* (a rest house or the abode of *Dharma*) to commemorate his visit to Kurukshetra, wherein God's name could be recited. *"Sat Kartar"* became their new salutation. This was an auspicious beginning to the Guru's campaign of spiritual conquest of the world.

At Hardwar

The Guru's next stop was at Hardwar, one of the holiest places in the entire 'Hindudom'. This pilgrimage spot of utmost beauty is situated where the Ganga enters the plains. It is always full of pilgrims who come here in the belief that consigning ashes of their dead to the Ganga releases the souls of the departed on the pathway to heaven.

On arriving there, the Guru took his seat at Kushaghat where thousands of people were making water offerings to quench the thirst of their forefathers. On seeing them throwing the water towards the sun with their right hand, the Guru started to throw the Ganga water towards the West with his left hand.

Taking him to be a plain rustic, a priest came forward and said, "May I help you to perform the ritual in the right way?"

"I am doing just as you are doing," and saying this, he continued doing as before.

"Well, we are offering water to the departed to quench the thirst of their souls."

"If so, then I am offering the Ganga water to quench the thirst of my parched lands."

At this, the priests mocked him, "How could this water reach your fields?" they asked.

Soon enough, a large crowd gathered there. The Guru addressing that concourse said, "If the water I am throwing cannot reach my fields which are on this very earth, then how come their water reaches their ancestors who are no more on this earth?"

"We have the power of the *mantras* on our side. What power is on your side?"

The Guru now decided to take priests head on. He said, "You trade on the credulity of these simple folks. You know that your *mantras* have no such power. You are sure to be punished for beguiling these simple folks." The game of the priests was up and, therefore, they thought it prudent to melt away.

Thereafter, the Guru took his seat among the pilgrims who had become his disciples. At the place where he sat, is situated *Nanakbara* (The enclosure of Nanak) which his disciples built in the memory of the Guru.

A new disciple of his now asked the Guru, "What is superstition?"

Nanak said that he could demonstrate it. Then he approached a Brahmin who had drawn a circle round him and was cooking his food. "May I enter your circle to take some firewood?"

"Get away. If you enter the circle, you will pollute my food."

The Guru said, "See, this is superstition. This Brahmin believes that by drawing a circle around him, he is keeping impurities away from him. But what can be more polluting than the evil-mindedness that resides in his heart?"

At Prayag

When the Guru reached Prayag, the *Kumbh* fair was on. He took his seat at the *Sangam* — the confluence of the Ganga, the Jamuna and the mythical Saraswati. At the auspicious hour, a great multitude bathed in the *Sangam*. But Nanak refrained. This shocked a Mahant who admonished the Guru for wasting the opportunity of a life-time.

"What opportunity?" asked Nanak.

"The opportunity of washing away your sins."

The Guru sang:

> "They are not pure who wash their bodies.
> They indeed are pure in whose heart dwells He."

And he continued singing while a big crowd gathered.

An interesting event took place then. A Pandit sat in front of a *chowky* (a low wooden stool) with many idols placed on it. He pretended to close his eyes, but watched the offerings carefully. So, Nanak asked him what he saw when he closed the eyes. The Pandit replied, "I see all the three worlds."

Nanak smiled and decided to teach the Pandit a lesson and asked Mardana to hide the Pandit's *chowky*. When the Pandit did not see his *chowky*, he was greatly upset. Then he asked Nanak if he knew who had stolen his *chowky*. At that Nanak asked him, "Why don't you close your eyes and find out."

The Pandit had got the message and with tears in his eyes, pleaded with the Guru not to torment him. The Guru said, "Why do you deceive others for a few coins? Collect the wealth of the sacred **Nam**. For that alone will help you save yourself as also others. Listen:

> *"He indeed is a fool*
> *Whose mind thirsts for money,*
> *Who laments when money is lost.*
> *Only the rare ones gather the true wealth —*
> *The wealth of the sacred **Nam**.*

> *"Inspired with true devotion,*
> *They are drenched in the colour of the sacred **Nam**.*
> *They offer their mind and soul to God*
> *And take refuge in Him."*

At Kashi

From Prayag, the Guru reached Kashi, known as the city of Lord Shiva. It is believed that anyone dying there wins immediate release from the cycle of birth and death. Attracted by his dress which identified him neither with the Hindus and nor with the Muslims, some Pandits came to hold discussions with him out of curiosity. The Guru asked, "Panditji, how does a sinner by merely dying in Kashi attain salvation?"

They answered, "Whoever touches the garment of Shiva is rendered pure. He does not remain a sinner once he reaches Kashi."

"Does anyone who listens to the Patanjali's *Yoga Sutra*, become a *Yogi* and acquire powers?" asked the Guru.

"No. One has to practise Yoga for long years before becoming a *Yogi*," was the answer.

"Does it not follow then that salvation cannot be attained by merely dwelling in a particular place?"

The Pandits were confused. They wanted to know more.

The Guru then explained, "Mere lip-service is of little avail. You cannot grasp the real meanings of words by merely reading them. Besides, you ignite fires of desire in many more ways; sowing the seeds of fresh *Karmas*.

Guru Nanak in one of his sessions with the Hindu anchorites on the banks of the Rameshwaran.

However, you make no attempt to be with Him, which you can do by serving His creation. In fact, you cling to a carcass without life."

Then the Guru taught the Pandits the right way by singing the following hymn:

> "Worshipping a stone God,
> Displaying a rosary of sacred beads,
> Is like watering a barren soil.
> Why waste life in empty formalities
> And plaster the body from outside
> When it is crumbling from inside?
>
> ....
>
> ....
>
> "The deeper you dig, the greater will be the harvest.
> Thus learn the art of spiritual husbandry.
> Honest labour earns its reward.
> Even a heron by divine grace can become a swan.
> Thus prays Nanak, Your humble devotee,
> Bestow Your bounty, O Bountiful One."

"You speak as if you have read all the *Veda*s and *Shastra*s. Have you?"

The Guru gave his reply in another hymn as under:

"A man may carry a cartload of books
He may have books all around him,
He may carry the books in boatloads,
Or fill empty caves with books.
He may read books for months and years,
He may read them throughout his life,
Till breath leaves his body.
Nanak says: Only one word is of consequence;
All else is for the glory of self."

Thereafter, a group of *Sanyasi*s invited the Guru to join them. He replied them in yet another hymn that contained a damning denunciation of the runaways of life. This hymn is as follows:

"In ignorance they leave their homes
And then visit the homes of others.
Having run away from the duties of a householder,
They are lost in the whirlpool of desire.
Without meeting a true teacher,
They wander about and read books,
Whetting the edge of desire,
Without the knowledge of the Word
And remain unprepared."

At Gaya

From Kashi, the Guru reached Gaya, the place where Lord Buddha had found enlightenment. It had become a place for making offerings for the absolution of forefathers.

The Guru stood at the banks of the sacred Saryu and watched people make the offerings. Then, he started laughing. A priest asked him what he was laughing at. In reply, the Guru said, "Do you mean that those who have left this body need food?"

"The food offered here, does reach them. But why don't you do the son's duty unto your forefathers and do what the others are doing?" the priest asked him.

At that, the Guru sang the following hymn:

"Brimful with the oil of suffering is the lamp (of life).
Kindle the flame of the sacred **Nam**.
The flame of the sacred **Nam**
Will consume the oil of suffering,
And the Lord Himself will be seen.
Don't you O people scoff at what I say:
A spark can ignite and consume
Logs stacked in thousands.
The rice balls placed on a leafy platter,
Of what avail can they be?"

Guru Nanak explaining to a priest the futility of making offerings for the absolution of forefathers, at the banks of the Saryu.

The priests were visibly annoyed with Nanak. They called him an ignorant rustic. However, they refused to enter into a debate with him.

In the end, the Guru questioned them: "When the material body is no more, how can it require material things? If the body cannot go to the other side, how can a material do so?"

"What should be the right thing to do?", the pilgrims asked him.

Nanak said, "Make a boat of the sacred *Nam* and row it with the oars of faith to be able to cross the ocean of illusion."

At Jagannath Puri

Guru Nanak's next halt was at Jagannath Puri where stands the world-famous temple of the 'Lord of the Universe', the literal meaning of the name Jagannath. When the Guru reached there, it was time for the evening service. As soon as it was dark, priests and pilgrims began to perform the *Aarti* (Prayer) of the Lord by burning incense, blowing conches, ringing the bells and waving lamps, carried in a salver. However, the Guru did not move. "Are you ill?" inquired a priest, approaching him when the service was over. "Why did you not join in offering the *Aarti* to the Lord of the Universe?"

"Where is the Lord of the Universe?" asked the Guru.

"Are you blind? Is the statute of the Lord not before you?"

"Not me but you are blind. Otherwise, tell me how can a statute of wood represent the Lord of the Universe?"

There were some hot words heaped upon the Guru by the priests and pilgrims alike. But the Guru was firm. He said, "I speak the truth. The Lord of the Universe resides in every human heart. He pervades all and the whole universe worships Him. He is unknowable — the Creator. I perform His *Aarti* alone. "

And saying this, the Guru began singing the *Aarti* of the Lord with Mardana giving him company on the *rabab*. The Guru's world-famous *Aarti* is as follows:

> *"In the salver of the sky,*
> *The sun and the moon are the lamps;*
> *The luminous stars are the pearls*
> *The warm wind from the Malaya mountain*
>   *wafts the* Chanwar
> *The forests of the world offer their wealth of flowers;*
> *And the spheres play their music.*
> *Thus is Your evening service performed,*
> *O Destroyer of the suffering!*
>
> ....
>
> ....
>
> *"What is pleasing to You*
> *Is the best of the evening service.*
> *Day and night my heart thirsts like the bumblebee*
> *To touch the dust of Your lotus-feet."*

After singing the *Aarti* thus, the Guru walked out of the temple with the whole multitude following. People grew thirsty. There was no fresh water available anywhere. The Guru then asked Mardana to dig up a hole in the earth where he stood. And unbelievable as it was, a spring of sweet water gushed forth from that hole. That spring still exists reminding us of the Guru's visit. The Sikhs later built a *Dharmasala* around that spring.

Visiting the Lake Mansarovar with a Lama

However, a very special part of the *Udasi*s of Guru Nanak was his visit to a Lamaserie in Ladakh precedent to his visit to the Mansarovar in the interior Himalayas. He was received by the Head Lama with due courtesies. The Lama then inquired "They say that in the plains below, many creeds are prevalent. Now, what are your views about the creation of the world as also of the Creator?"

The Guru described his belief in the following hymn:

"From the soundless Absolute proceeds everything.
He the soundless emanates sound
And from it flows forth air, water, fire, light and souls.
He, the Absolute, remains unaffected and
  yet maintains all that lives.
He the Lord of the creation rejoices in His own creation.
The Absolute produces Brahma, Vishnu and Shiva
And also time and the four great ages.
He who knows the Absolute as all-pervading
Is a perfect man, and in his company
  is destroyed the delusion."

"Yes, it is quite logical. But please tell me more about it," the Lama said.

The Guru said, "The light of the Absolute pervades the three worlds. The Absolute is limitless; the Absolute is *Samadhi* itself. When the human mind, by the power of the Word as communicated by his Guru, bathes in the lake of truth, it obtains release from the wheel of births and deaths."

The Lama was thankful to the Guru because it tallied with what the Buddha had taught to the world. Therefore, he said, "So the truth of Lord Buddha still holds good that all beings are tied to the wheel and so suffer agonies till they earn release by following the eight-fold path."

Finally, the Lama asked, "Can a philosopher break the bonds of attachment?"

"No, an emphatic no. It is only the true Guru who awakens the *Buddhi* (intellect that controls the mind) and opens the door that leads to realization. Then the pure sound of the true word is heard and the **Nam** enters the heart which makes for pure *Samadhi.*"

"How can we reach the Absolute?" The Lama asked highly pleased.

The Guru said, "The Absolute is in you. It is the light that resides in each heart. But it is discovered under the instruction of a true Guru."

At last the Lama asked, "Why does pain haunt those that work for pleasure?"

The Guru was pleased with the question and said, "Pain is nothing but the reflex of pleasure itself. When we seek pleasure, we automatically court pain. The only way to escape pain, therefore, is to quench the thirst of pleasure."

The Guru and the Lama then headed together for the lake Mansarovar. They passed through dense deserts of virgin snows. At last, braving all impediments, they met great ascetics, mahatmas, renouncers of every description, and evolved souls who weilded enormous supernatural attainments. When they came to know that Nanak was from India, they felt hugely excited.

"In what condition is your land?" They asked as if in one voice.

"Why do you ask me?" asked Nanak, "You all know that the dark age of *Kaliyuga* is upon us and it is like a knife which the kings brandish like butchers. Justice has taken wings and flown away. The darkness of untruth obscures the light of the moon. Humanity is groaning under the dreaded domination of self. And yet the falsehood must fail and truth alone prevail."

These words of the Guru electrified the whole atmosphere and with one voice they said, "Hail! Hail to Nanak!"

In reply the Guru said, "Hail! Hail to Him! Hail to the Lord of all!"

Then the Guru passed into utter ecstasy and sang the following hymn:

> *"He is the True One*
> *There is no other.*
> *He sends forth the universe*
> *And absorbs it in Himself as it pleases Him.*
>
> *"He is the creator of the three* gunas.
> *He drives us to action and bondage,*
> *He Himself is all wisdom,*
> *He Himself is the knower*
> *He Himself is ever satisfied."*

This beautiful hymn summed up the whole truth. The great conclave of the evolved ones needed no more discussion and explanation. They all exulted in the glory of the living Guru and enjoyed his company. And on this victorious note ended the spiritual conquest of the known world of religion of the time. This odyssey of Nanak took more than two decades.

Guru Nanak by the lake Manasarovar addressing spiritual questions put to him by some of the leading savants of the world when he undertook a long journey with the Head Lama. 41

Doing Business with a Banker

A rich banker in Nasik was out to impress the Guru in various ways, particularly by flaunting his enormous riches. He had heard the Guru sing the following lines:

> *"The whole world is full of pain.*
> *He alone is happy in whose heart dwells the **Nam**."*

In essence, the Guru knew that the banker was a very unhappy man. So, he decided to cure him of his lure of gold and money. The Guru spoke, "I need nothing from you. Yet, I have a favour to ask of you if you can oblige," he said to the banker.

This flattered the banker beyond measure. He said, "Anything, anything you name and I shall do. I am entirely at your service."

The Guru continued, "You are a leading banker. All I want to do is to keep this small needle in good trust and have it returned when we meet in the next life."

The banker laughed and said, "You are truly naïve. How can we carry anything to the next life?"

Now it was the Guru's turn to laugh. "Who is really being naïve, you or I? You are gathering wealth which you cannot carry anywhere with you, while I am seeking what shall go with me."

The banker fell at the Guru's feet.

He had now learnt the importance of using money for those who needed it, and kept just enough for his family's subsistence.

Setting up the Commune at Kartarpur

Guru Nanak, during his long *Udasis*, moved from village to village and town to town, covering Punjab, the land of his birth and the main field of his activity, many times over. It was during those itinerant days that he also founded Kartarpur, which was to be the future headquarter of his movement. The story runs like this:

Once while travelling in Punjab, Nanak came to stay at a place on the banks of the Ravi for some length of time. Here, all kinds of people, Hindus, and Muslims, *Sadhus* and *Fakirs*, paupers and kings, flocked to hear him sing morning hymns and evening prayers in his mellifluous voice, apart from spiritual instructions. The news that spread all over was that wherever the Guru stayed, falsehood found no place and truth was proclaimed. And, so the site became especially blessed.

However, the site belonged to a rich and cynical Muslim landlord, popularly called Karoria. That an infidel should become so popular, staying on his land, excited his jealousy no end. Besides, the Guru was preaching something that the fundamental Islam did not permit. So, he decided to ask the Guru to pack up from there and set up his camp elsewhere.

Accordingly, he gathered some armed guards and mounting his horse set out for the Guru's camp. But he had hardly gone some distance when his horse stumbled and he fell headlong. After taking rest for a few days, he continued his mission. But he had barely left the gates when he realised that he could not see clearly. He, therefore, dismounted and returned to his house, wondering why such unusual things were happening to him! As soon as he started to move in the direction of his house, he began to see things clearly once again.

"What is it that is happening to me?" Karoria asked his followers.

"Nanak is a holy man," they said, "And you are going there with the intention of expelling him. It has not pleased God. So, he has not allowed you to proceed with your intention."

"I will show him all respect," saying this, he mounted his horse once again. But he had hardly gone a few paces when he felt the same problem with his eyesight. "What am I to do now?" he asked his followers ruefully.

"Sir, you must go on foot," said his followers. "Purge your heart of anger and humbly beg for his forgiveness before starting."

The rich and cynical landlord Karoria experiencing blindness while on his way to have Nanak ousted from his land.

Thus, Karoria, humbly praying to be forgiven started his journey on foot. And his eyes did not let him down. And so, he reached the place where the Guru had taken abode.

The Guru was sitting calmly, surrounded by all kinds of people. Sweet music was wafting in all directions. This filled Karoria with an incredible sense of peace. He instantly fell at the Guru's feet who, in turn, embraced him affectionately and made him sit next to him.

After a moment, Karoria stood up and bowed his head saying, "I am truly blessed by the sight of you, O Master! I know I have been forgiven. Kindly permit me to dedicate this entire area to you. You can now found a new settlement here as you please."

Accepting the offer, the Guru said, "All land belongs to Kartar (the Maker) and you are indeed blessed for dedicating it for a divine purpose. From now on, we shall know this place as Kartarpur, the seat of the Creator."

Soon, Sikhs from all over started building *Dharmasalas* (inns) and houses there. The Guru too shifted his family to Kartarpur.

Thus, Kartarpur became the seat of the Guru where the congregation started growing by the day. All the inmates of the place were now fed from the common kitchen. Not just that, the Guru set up a small farm there that he cultivated himself. In fact, all inmates were required to earn their own bread the hard, honest way. Besides, it was a simple householder's life that was the path applicable to them and the principal message of this path was that all divinity lived in the family.

Chapter V

Some Gems of Nanak's Spiritual Message

After his historic encounter with Babur in 1521, the Guru had settled at Kartarpur where he spent the last 19-20 years of his life. These were the years of his mature thought. In addition, he had to spend most of his time in consolidating all that he had done in his four *Udasi*s. His Sikhs, spread far and wide, were now quite numerous and hence needed an organization on a more permanent footing.

The Guru thus devoted a good amount of his energy to this task as well. Many well-to-do disciples who also built their quarters at Kartarpur helped the Guru establish a full-fledged commune there that also emerged as his profound study circle. In effect, if all that the Guru did at Kartarpur is put together, it must form a veritable compendium of spiritual gems of the type the sages of yore dished out on God, soul, cosmos, man, ideal living, death and how to earn salvation.

The daily routine at Kartarpur as described in the *Sakhi*s is something like this: The Guru and disciples rose before dawn, known as *Amrit vela* or the ambrosial hour. Then, they cleaned their bodies and minds as best as possible and getting together recite the *Japuji* and the Asa-di-Var. It was followed by choral singing or *Kirtan* and the expounding of hymns as led by the Guru.

Guru Nanak working in his farm at Kartarpur where everyone was enjoined to work for his/her living.

After greeting the morning with a happy spirit, everybody, including the Guru got down to serious work. Farming took top priority. Then, as evening fell, the *Rehra*s was recited followed by the *Aarti*. They sung the *Sohila* before retiring to bed.

But the most important part of the activity was that of the study circle in which the Guru answered the spiritual questions that bothered the Sikhs. As the Guru sat on a cot, all types of questions were fielded in the spirit of true inquiry and answers came from the Guru's vast repertoire of spiritual experience. However, we begin the life at Kartarpur with a story of Bhai Buddha who later was known as Baba Buddha. This story is as under:

Old Head on Young Shoulders

Guru Nanak accepting the very young Baba Buddha as his disciple. who went on to become a virtual institution in the growing Sikh Church and was later appointed by Guru Arjan as the Head Granthi of Harmandir Sahib after the installation of Guru Granth Sahib in it in 1604.

Bhai Buddha was about seven when he started participating in the commune's activity at Kartarpur. On the first day, the Guru, full of curiosity, asked him, "What brings you here?" The answer was, "It is you, O my Guru, who call me." Then by way of explanation, he said, "One day my mother asked me to light a fire. I learnt that little sticks caught the fire before the big ones. It made me realise that I was ready to get ignited by knowledge. Hence, I decided to prepare myself for my journey to the other world right now."

46

"You speak like an old man. You indeed are wise. I shall, therefore, call you Bhai Buddha (an old man)." Then getting into an ecstatic mood, the Guru began to sing:

> "A fish swimming in the deep water,
> Wise and beautiful and all too trusting
> Does not realise that it may fall in the fisherman's net;
> Tempted by desire it walks into the noose of death.
> Brother! Realise that death is lurking just round
>   the corner,
> And like the fish a man may fall into its noose any time.
> The whole world is subject to a time-limit.
> Only the Guru is beyond its limit."

Now we bring together some of the questions asked by the inquisitive disciples and the answers as provided by the Guru:

God's command and Man's free will

One day, a Sikh asked the Guru, "When we act under His command it means we have no free will of our own. And if that's the case, then how can we seek salvation?"

The Guru said, "I have repeated many times that God's **Nam** has the power of releasing the seeker from the bondage of *Karma*s. But it is again by His grace alone that this secret is known. Our acts are invariably attended by their fruits as long as I-amness rules. Free will is exercised only when we become free of I-amness."

How Does the *Jiva-atma* Sin?

A Sikh well-versed in philosophy asked the Guru, "What is the origin of sin? How can the *Jiva-atma* (soul) sin when it is divine in essence?"

The Guru said, "There are many things that elude its definition. The root of things are known to Him alone who created this universe. For us, it is enough to know that we commit sin. We do so when we quench our thirst for things by trampling over the rights of others. When we trespass the law of love, punishment is inevitable."

The questioner further asked, "Who is the real performer? For, it cannot be the soul. How is then the divine soul bound to the wheel of birth and death?"

The Guru said, "The divinity of soul is infinite; it is beyond human comprehension. On the plane of action, we know that hope and desire rule the mind. Hence, actions prompted by these make for bondage. The world is born of good and bad deeds. He who fails to take shelter in God is under their spell and hence is perishable."

The same questioner continued the discussion. He asked, "How does the *Maya* (illusion born of ignorance) enamour the mind and turn it into a slave?"

The Guru replied, "The dictates of mind are translated into the will to act. It is the mind that conceives good and bad actions. Intoxicated with sense objects, the mind never finds rest. It can be happy only when it turns to the True One."

The Mystery of Dreams

"O Satguru! Kindly explain to us the mystery of dreams," asked another Sikh. "For, isn't it in the dreams that one sees without the eyes and hears without the ears? Also, in dreams, the dead walk with the living. Not just that, in a dream the sun and the moon, do not exist to mark time. Besides, in a dream, even future happenings are foreseen."

The Guru said, "Dreams bear witness to the fact that sense organs are the only vehicles the soul uses on the physical plane. On a higher plane, however, the soul sees, hears and acts without its physical instruments. Hence, the barriers of time and physical death do not intervene between the living and the dead. Past, present and future are transparent in a higher state of consciousness."

Elaborating further, the Guru said, "In sleep, the day turns into unreality. Similarly on awakening, the dreams become

Nanak explaining to other Sikhs the mystery of dreams.

48

unreal. In deep sleep, both this world and the dream world cease to exist. Which means the consciousness becomes aware of its own self. We dream when consciousness is a witness to outer impressions. When we are awake, we are aware of the existence of the world. When consciousness retires into itself, beyond the bounds of waking and dreaming, nothing exists."

The Three *Gunas* (Qualities)

"What are the three *Gunas*?" asked another Sikh.

The Guru said, "*Gunas* are the aspects of energy. The grosser aspect of energy is *Tamas* (Darkness); the active aspect of energy is *Rajas* (that works for action, progress and achievement); and *Satva* is the purest aspect of energy that works for elevating the mind towards the divine." And then sang:

Guru Nanak explaining the importance of serving those in need of help and thus finding oneself closer to God.

> "In surrendering to You O Master!
> Hope and desire have vanished,
> The domination of the three Gunas is at an end,
> Having taken shelter with You, Your devotee,
> With the favour of the Guru, has gained the turiya
>   (supra-conscious) state."

"Satguru! What is it that always lives and never dies?" asked yet another Sikh.

"That which is not subject to the three *gunas*, for example, the matter that partakes of the three *gunas* and undergoes changes. As against it, the soul that gives life is changeless. He alone lives in whose heart He dwells. None else is really alive."

The same disciple asked, "Why is this *Jiva* born and why does it die again and again?"

The Guru answered, "The *Jiva* inspired by the will persists in affirming the Self. Self-assertion is the disease; self-surrender is the cure."

Serving the Needy is Service of God

A Sikh approached the Guru and asked for his forgiveness. He was in great hurry. "Satguru!" he said, I am attending upon a friend of mine who has been ailing. I had to leave him in the morning because I could not miss the sight of your august presence.

Visibly angry, the Guru said, "You have ignored my teachings by coming to me to serve yourself rather than serving the one whom God has placed in your care. Remember! It is more important to nurse your friend back to health than what I teach here."

When that Sikh departed, the Guru observed, "See how the self intrudes upon men of good intentions. Indeed, until the self melts into God-consciousness, there is no freedom

49

from the gratification of the self." Then the Guru started singing:

"The light of dawn breaks forth when the ego dies.
Then the tide of goodwill for all fills the heart.
He who sees himself in all that exists,
He indeed is exalted, says Nanak."

Gurmukh and *Manmukh*

Once, an inquisitive Sikh asked the Guru, "You always say that a *Gurmukh* is exalted and a *Manmukh* remains bankrupt. Pray, tell us what you mean by that and how to distinguish a *Gurmukh* from a *Manmukh*."

The Guru said, "One who is holy and righteous is *Gurmukh*. He always lives in the state of happiness. Not just that, he gives happiness to others. As to how to distinguish one from the other, it is to be done by watching their actions. For example, a *Gurmukh* is pleased at hearing the praise of others. He serves the poor and the needy. He is respectful towards the virtuous and the learned. He avoids discussing subjects that can give rise to quarrels. He protects the rights of others and does not trample upon them. His pure intentions are reflected in being faithful to his wife, respectful to other women and to be in the company of holy men. His craving for the **Nam** grows by the day."

Another Sikh asked the Guru, "How can one become a *Gurmukh*?"

The Guru said, "It is not easy. However, it is not difficult either. To be a *Gurmukh* one must avoid the *Manmukh karma*."

"What is the *Manmukh karma*?" the whole congregation asked.

"A *Manmukh* is basically jealous of everyone. Not just that, he regards all men as his enemies and hates them. He covets all the worldly wealth and happiness for himself so much so that he wants everyone else to be poor and unhappy and that all their wealth should come to him. He suffers great pain when he sees other people's houses, property and other good things of life."

Finding Happiness in the World

A jeweller who was listening to all this with rapt attention asked the Guru, "Tell me how to find happiness in the world."

The Guru said, "He alone is happy who knows the truth. Having subdued the ego and with it the thirst for things, a happy man remains absorbed in the truth."

"What happens to those who do not realise the truth?" the jeweller asked further.

A rare painting of Guru Nanak as the
King of King's even as a *Dervish*.

"One who does not realise the truth, burns in the fire of desire. But one who knows his own self, becomes one with the infinite God."

The jeweller then asked yet another question, "What are the characteristics of a good man?"

"A good man," said the Guru, "does not wrap himself in indifference. He returns good for evil and his heart is empty of hate and envy. He suffers when the others suffer; he is happy when others are happy."

Who is a Devotee?

"What are the characteristics of a devotee?" asked a Sikh.

The Guru said, "A devotee is like a virgin bride who surrenders herself to the bridegroom without any thought of self. A devotee is no more aware of his separate self when in the service of the Beloved (God). The image of the beloved fills his heart till all sense of separateness departs and the devotee becomes one with the object of his devotion."

Who is a Sikh?

"Tell us, O Master! What are the characteristics of a true Sikh?" another Sikh asked.

"A Sikh is he who is truthful, contented and compassionate towards all. He is free from covetousness and hate. He is harmless, dispassionate and desireless. He is self-controlled and has learnt to discriminate. He surrenders himself to the Supreme God and learns to abide by His will. Such a one has truly entered the path of my discipleship."

The *Nam* or the True Word and how it Possesses the Mind

One day, Muni Lal, a noted Sikh of the Guru asked him, "O Satguru! You say that the sacred Word has the power to transmute suffering into bliss as also egoism into selflessness. But the question is, how is the true Word to possess the mind?"

Observed the Guru, "It is only when we win His favours by righteous living that we acquire the power to repeat the sacred *Nam*. It is then that the word reaches the *Jiva-atma* and lifts it to *Paramatma*. Then the two become one and duality is destroyed. It is through the grace of the Guru that this is known and the domain of death is left behind."

"It sounds so easy," said Muni Lal, "when you speak O Satguru! But the veil of darkness persists and refuses to be lifted."

"When we practise truth", said the Guru, "his light illuminates darkness and it no more clings to this poisonous world."

"Forgive me, O Satguru! But how can I practise truth to be worthy of the grace of the Guru?"

"It is by serving Him that we follow the path of truth and by surrendering to Him what is His. Such service pleases the Master and when accepted by Him, He bestows His grace," said the Guru.

"It is not easy to be attached to the invisible," said Muni Lal. "It is still more difficult to know how to serve Him when no direct service is rendered."

"To love His creation is to serve Him," said the Guru, "Instal the image of the Guru in your heart, then you will get what you desire. The true Lord with His grace accepts such a servant and removes the fear of death from his mind."

"How should one begin to shift the mind from worldly activities to divine activities?" asked Muni Lal.

"You must begin," said the Guru, "to meditate on truth and cultivate devotion to the Word. The fruit of recitation and austerities is hidden in the true Word; it leads you to the door of salvation."

Guru Nanak at Kartarpur with some Muslim disciples engaged in a group discussion on some intricate point of Sikh spirituality.

53

Cosmos and How it came into Existence

One day a learned Pandit, after attending the morning prayers, asked the Guru, "Kindly tell us how this world came into existence."

"How strange that we know nothing about our own coming on the earth and still want to know how the whole creation came into being!" exclaimed the Guru. Then he said, "You want to know at what time, in which epoch, on what lunar day and the day of the week or in which month, or in what season was this world created. If the Pandits had known it, they would have recorded it in the *Puranas*. Likewise, had the Prophet known it, he would have mentioned the same in the *Quran*. Then, the Guru started singing:

> *"For unlimited period there was darkness.*
> *There was neither heaven nor earth;*
> *There was only the boundless Word.*
> *There was neither the sun nor the moon,*
> *Nor was there day and night.*
> *He alone was in a state of* Samadhi.
> *There was no species nor speech, neither air nor water.*
> *No creation, nor its dissolution, nor birth nor death.*
> *Neither there were divisions of earth, nor of*
> *   the seven regions;*
> *Neither there were oceans, nor were the rivers,*
> *Nor was there the water flowing."*

What binds the Soul to the Wheel of Births and Deaths?

Similarly, one day a learned Brahmin adept in scholarly disputation came to Kartarpur and asked the Guru, "Tell us, O great Master! What binds the soul to the wheel of births and deaths. And besides, what is the cause of pleasure and pain?"

The Guru was amused by the pomposity of his learning. However, he said, "The pleasure and pain are the fruit of one's past *karma*s. And for this, a man can blame none but himself. Origin of the *karma*s is known to Him alone. Man, chained by hope and desire, brews venom that poisons him and others who come into his contact."

Further, the Brahmin asked, "How then to rid oneself of the bondage of action and the poison of one's own brewing?"

The Guru said, "He who purifies himself in the pool of truth and praises God, fills his consciousness with real love and makes himself one with God, if he remains no more entangled in the noose of births and deaths."

"But O Master! the heart does not throb with love and consciousness refuses to be one-pointed, then what should the seeker do?"

The Guru said, "Cultivate contentment, truthfulness and forgiveness. The Giver of gifts bestows the power to know yourself and in so doing acquire the knowledge of the universal Self. Only the unrighteous are condemned to be drowned in untruth and deceit."

"Teach us, O Guru! How to know this Self?"

"Five elements make the body. In it dwells the jewel of God," said the Guru. "Realize it. For, the *Jiva* is of God and one with God."

The True Path

One day, a party of *Sadhu*s came to Kartarpur and asked the Guru to show them the true path.

The Guru said, "The weak and wavering cannot follow the true path. We search what is pleasant and discard what is unpleasant. Those who talk are many. But only a rare one knows the meaning of renunciation."

The leader of the party wanted the Guru to tell them more. At that the Guru said, "With great travails we gather things of the world. But that does not appease the fire of hunger. The more it is fed, the more flames does it create. The demands of body for the enjoyment of dainties are only equalled by the suffering they cause."

The leader of the *Sadhu*s confessed that he was still a slave of five passions and then pleaded to the Guru to lead them to the light of all lights — the abode of eternal peace. Upon that the Guru started singing:

> *"This body is the temple of the Lord,*
> *In it dwells the infinite light.*
> *By the grace of the Guru is a disciple called*
> *To enter the inner temple to be one with Him."*

Guru Nanak sitting in a regal canopy in one of his *darbar*s at Kartarpur.

55

Shadow of the *Maya*

One day, the Guru was walking to the river Ravi followed by a band of disciples in the tradition of the commune. A disciple took courage and joining the Guru asked him, "How is it that we cannot dispel the illusion of *Maya*?"

The Guru said, "Just look at your shadow. You walk miles and miles and if the sun is behind, your shadow will always lie before you. But if you turn your face towards the sun . . ." and so saying, he turned the pupil to face the sun.

"Yes, it has disappeared," admitted the disciple.

"So, what do you deduce from it? You learn that as long as your face is turned away from God, the shadow of the *Maya* does not leave you. But the moment you turn your face towards God, all shadows of the *Maya* disappear."

"Then what prevents us from turning towards God?" asked the disciple.

"A man is born with the desire to become. And that's his undoing. It is only when he follows the right path that he secures his release by the power of the sacred **Nam**."

"It's not easy to follow the right path," several disciples said in chorus. "Then how should one prepare for the journey's end?"

"Seek the company of men in whose heart dwells God. Surrender your will to the Divine will. Then the wandering mind will cease to pursue the sense objects. It will turn from the unreal to the real."

"So, do you O Satguru!, suggest that we should perform the duties of the householder, without concentrating our minds on the performance?"

This question was after the Guru's heart's desire. He said, "Turn your minds towards God. When that happens, your heart will be with the Beloved while your hands will perform the act. The mind that is God-filled is only conscious of Him and unconscious of all else. And this state can be reached even as a householder, more easily than the renouncer."

"How is it possible?"

The Guru said, "Don't you look at the yonder river flowing without pause? Well, it is doing so under the divine law. Let your life also flow as the river does under the divine command. Thus place your body and mind at the service of the Lord and serve Him through pain and suffering."

Then another important question attracted the Guru's attention. A Sikh asked him, "Hindus and Muslims follow the law as given by their law-givers or prophets. But what is the law that the Sikhs should follow?"

"The law of truth," snapped the Guru. "For, falsehood fades away and truth alone prevails."

Breath-control and Mind-control

One day a Yogi, well-versed in *Hath* Yoga came to Kartarpur and asked the Guru, "O great Teacher! Pray tell me how inspite of my performing breath-control, my mind does not gain tranquillity? It wanders even in my meditation."

"The answer is simple" said the Guru, "You want to control the breath which is a physical action. Until the mind itself is washed clean, it can never be tranquil. But when the mind becomes tranquil, the breathing gets under control easily and the *Pranayam* results."

"They say that there are *nadi*s (channels of consciousness) of power within the body and these can be stirred through inhalation and exhalation. And this brings about breath control through which results mind control. By retaining the breath in the *Sushumana* (a *nadi* in *Hath* Yoga), the hidden serpent of *Kundalini* (another *nadi*) can be awakened."

Breath and mind control: Awakening of the *Kundalini*.

The Guru said to him with a smile, "You are well-versed in *Hath* Yoga. You have also discovered that these outer restraints cannot awaken the soul or secure salvation. However you may acquire super-natural powers. But these will perish along with the body."

"Is it true that the three *guna*s dominate man?" asked the Yogi.

"Yes," said the Guru, "*Guna*s are the aspects of the creative impulse that makes the world. The *Tamas* makes for material stability; the *Rajas* for progress; and the *Satva* for the return of the pure into the pure. If the *Tamas* and the *Rajas* dry up, the self is realized as the mind becomes one with God."

What do you know of the *Brahm*?

One day, a reputed *Gyani* came to the Guru to discourse with him on how to win salvation. The Guru heard him with great patience and then asked, "What do you know of the *Brahm*?"

"I know all that the *Veda*s and *Shastra*s tell us on the subject."

The Guru asked, "If salvation could be achieved through knowledge then you must have achieved it?"

The *Gyani* had no reply to this question. Finding him faltering, the Guru said, "Words are but symbols; reality must be mastered to obtain salvation."

"I know all this but I cannot rid myself of the limitations of my own self," confessed the *Gyani*.

The Guru said, "The feeling of separateness must vanish before one can have knowledge of Him. All humanity is conscious of its own existence. But only a few can abolish the barrier of I-amness to be able to become one with God."

When is the *Bhakti* Obtained?

One day the Guru was sitting on the banks of the Ravi. A Sikh fell into the river and was almost drowned when the Guru himself jumped into the river and rescued him. When the Sikh regained his consciousness, the Guru asked him, "Tell me, when you were going down what was it that was uppermost in your mind."

The Sikh said, "I had lost all consciousness. Yet, I desired one thing so very badly and that was breath."

To all those present the Guru then addressed, "When a man becomes unconscious of everything and desires God with all the power of being, he attains *Bhakti* or devotion. However, taste in the fish, sound in the snake, smell in the bee, passion for light in the moth, sense of touch in the elephant are desires of the senses that often become the cause of their destruction. Human beings are lured by not one but five senses to misguide us. Therefore, we must have only one object to desire for all the five senses. And in that desire fulfill all other desires.

Continuing the Guru said, "Most people profess to love others; a few indeed love them. But a true devotee of the Guru, a Sikh, must love all, even those who hate him. Similarly, the whole world works for gain. Only a rare one works without desire. But a Sikh must serve friends and foes alike, knowing that it is only thus that he can serve God."

In the same vein, the Guru said, "Most people want their names to be exalted. A few want their friends to be exalted. There are a few who desire neither name nor fame. But a Sikh of the Guru exalts the name of God."

58   Guru Nanak receiving some Muslim nobleman at Kartarpur.

Getting ready to return to the Eternal Home

One day Pir Baha-ud-Din of Multan came to meet the Guru at Kartarpur. The purpose of his visit was to bid goodbye to his old spiritual friend before bowing out. The Guru welcomed him with open arms.

The venerable Pir said, "My boat is now loaded and is ready to take to the unknown seas. Can you help me to lighten the load?"

The Guru did not speak for a long time. In the end, he said, "Dear friend, we carry the sack we have sedulously filled. But His mercy and grace alone can lighten the load of those who empty their hearts of self and stand at His door for forgiveness."

The Pir and the Guru remained silent for a long time, communicating with each other in the wordless language known only to the men of God. In the end, the Guru broke the silence, saying, "I also feel I have fulfilled my mission and must now return home. I am happy that the day is drawing near."

Naming the Successor

The Sikh movement had now become an all-India brotherhood. It had teachings sourced in God Himself. It had a large and focussed membership, neither Hindu nor Muslim. Now, it needed a new Guru so that Nanak's work could continue after him.

Let us, therefore, see how Nanak chose his successor, Guru Angad or Nanak II. The first important thing to know is that he deprived his two sons from succession. He did so to select one who could keep the Sikh mission and its values intact. His sons, though gifted, did not measure up to his expectations.

Lehna was a Khatri of the Trehan clan. He was born in 1504 AD. His circumstances were far from congenial and forced him to shift from his native village in Ferozepur district to Khadur in Amritsar district, where his in-laws lived. Lehna was a great devotee of the Mother. He would undertake regular pilgrimages to Jwalamukhi, the Mother of the Flaming Mouth in the Kangra hills, and Chintpurni, the Mother who is known to grant the wishes of all her devotees, in the Hoshiarpur district.

One day, he heard a neighbour sing some hymns of Guru Nanak. He was greatly influenced by the spiritual message of these hymns. Not long after, he visited Kartarpur. There, he heard the Guru's discourses, followed the strict religious regimen of the inmates and participated in all activities of

Guru Nanak accepting Lehna as his disciple. It is Lehna who became Angad Dev and rose to be the second Sikh lord after Nanak.

the commune with such devotion that he never left the feet of the Guru thereafter. Thus, in a short while, he had made a special place for himself and was considered a Sikh of the finest order along with Bhai Buddha.

But before he became the next Guru, he had to pass through some rigorous tests of loyalty to the Master. From the last test, we can infer what kind of tests these were. They say that after behaving like a mad man for some time, Nanak one day led his Sikhs to a cremation ground. When they reached there it was afternoon and the Sikhs were feeling hungry. So, the Guru invited them to share a special dish he had for them. Then pointing to a putrid dead body covered with a sheet, he said, "Eat it."

The disciples were greatly shocked. So, they started melting away one by one but not Bhai Lehna. When he was left alone, he asked the Guru, "From which side should I begin eating, my Guru?" When Lehna removed the sheet covering the dead body to get on with the job, his Master's face lit up. He had found a worthy successor. Then embracing Bhai Lehna, the Guru said, "From now on, you shall cease to be Bhai Lehna. You are Angad Dev — the limb of my limb. You are me." Thus Bhai Lehna became Guru Angad.

Final Audieu

The story of Nanak's departure from the world is equally interesting. It is like this:

After anointing Guru Angad as his successor in a gaily decorated *Diwan* and bowing before him as Nanak incarnate, the Guru left his residence and sat under a tree which suddenly burst into green foliage. This was a signal of the things to come.

The news that the Guru had decided to cast off his worldly frame in no time spread far and wide. The Sikhs flocked round him from all directions. The Guru sat unperturbed and as usual spoke to the congregation. He said that his mission having been fulfilled, he was now returning to the abode of his Maker and that they should rejoice at it.

Then he led them all to sing:

> *"Hail to the Creator, the true king, who allotted to the*
> *world its various duties.*
> *When the measure is full, the duration of life is at an end,*
> *the soul is led away;*
> *When the destined hour arrives, the soul is led away and*
> *all one's relatives weep.*
> *The body and the soul are separated O my Mother,*
> *when one's days are at an end."*

Hindus and Muslims removing the sheet to uncover the Guru's body and discovering a heap of flowers in its place.

After that, the Guru fell into a trance. When that trance broke, he saw his two sons weeping. He consoled them. Then he asked the Sikhs to sing the *Sohila*. The crowd sang the *Sohila* and concluded with the last verse of the *Japuji*. Thereafter, the Guru drew a white sheet over him. They say that at that time flowers dropped from the heaven and celestial beings started singing heavenly tunes.

The Guru passed away on the 10th day of the light half of the month of *Asuj* (corresponding to September 22).

Immediately, a dispute of sorts arose between the Hindu and Muslim followers of the Guru. The Hindus wanted to cremate the mortal remains of their Guru and the Muslims, bury them as their Pir. But when the sheet that covered the dying Guru was lifted, his body was to be found nowhere. In the end, that sheet was cut into two equal halves — one taken by the Hindu and Sikh devotees and the other by the Muslims followers.

And soon these words were sung all over Punjab:

> *"Baba Nanak Shah Fakir;*
> *Hindu ka Guru, Mussalman ka Pir."*

(The old Nanak is both a king and a *fakir*. For, even though he rules all lands, he owns nothing. He is common to both the Hindus and the Muslims. While to the Hindus, he is their Guru, to the Muslims, he is their Pir.)

This commonness of Guru Nanak between the Hindus and the Muslims greatly impressed Akbar, the Great.

Nanak's unique immortality begins with his physical exit from the world in 1539 AD. The story that follows is one of nine consecutive rebirths of none other than Nanak himself. This story can be best understood in two parts: The first part pertains to eight rebirths of Nanak i.e. from 1539 AD to 1675 AD. And the second part pertains to his ninth rebirth i.e. from 1675 AD to 1708 AD. The Sikh lore symbolically puts it as *"Ek Jot; Ek Jugat"*. Translated, it means, 'one spark and one style'.

In the first 136 years whatever Nanak had left behind by way of his spiritual legacy underwent a unique consolidation in the shape of a new and dynamic religion called Sikhism complete with a Messiah, a Book and a Church. And in the second period of 33 years, there took place a transformation so extraordinary that nothing like it has taken place in any church before or since.

For a better understanding of the first part, we have again divided it into two halves. The first half pertains to the first four Gurus after Nanak, which we have called the pacifist mode of Sikhism. The second half pertains to the next four Gurus e.g. from the sixth to the ninth Guru, which we have called as the martial mode of

Guru Nanak with all his nine successors along with Bala and Mardana. Sitting to Nanak's right are: Guru Angad, Guru Amar Das, Guru Ram Das, Guru Arjan and Guru Hargobing. To his left are: Guru Har Rai, Guru Har Kishan, Guru Tegh Bahadur and Guru Gobind Singh. Mardana and his companion Bala are sitting directly opposite Nanak.

Sikhism. It is remarkable that both these modes end in the Gurus earning martyrdoms of the most luminous kind.

The second part is confined wholly to the ministry of the Tenth Nanak, Guru Gobind Singh. It is during these thirty-three years that the Guru gave birth to the Khalsa.

Now let us know something of the first part:

Consolidation of the Sikh Church

The period of 136 years from September 7, 1539 (when Guru Angad became the second Nanak) to November 11, 1675 (when Guru Tegh Bahadur, the ninth Nanak left for his heavenly abode), is remarkable in the annals of Sikhism. During this period two epochmaking events took place: (1) Consolidation of the Nanak panth into a full-fledged theocratic but tolerant and eclectic church; and (2) the two extremely luminous martyrdoms that shook the conscience of India as never before. In fact, it is these 136 years that made the Sikh church 'a State within a State' and a contender for political power.

The first half, as we have already known, is dominated by the *Bhakti* mode of Sikhism. It ends with the martyrdom of Guru Arjan or the fifth Nanak. Thereafter starts what we know as the martial or *Shakti* mode of Sikhism. This mode ends with the martyrdom of Guru Tegh Bahadur or the Ninth Nanak. It is during the second mode that the Sikhs started arming themselves in defense against the tyranny and persecution of the State.

The *Bhakti* Mode (1539 AD to 1606 AD)

The main events of this period are as under:

Guru Angad, the second Nanak, ascended the throne of Nanak on September 7, 1539. He guided the destinies of the mission for almost 13 years.

Like Nanak, he too was an inspired poet. 63 of his *shloka*s find place in the Guru Granth Sahib. He perfected the *Gurmukhi* script so that he could supply to the *sangat*s authentic copies of the *Bani* of his Master. He also collected the events and legends connected with the life of Nanak. For that, he is said to have invited Bala Sandhu, a life-long companion of Guru Nanak and encouraged him to pen down what came to be known as *Bhai Bale vali Sakhi* or the witness account of Nanak's life by Bala Sandhu.

Another main contribution of Guru Angad is the strengthening of Sikh institutions. He was particularly devoted to the institution of free kitchen or *Guru ka Langar*. It is remarkable that while his wife cooked, the Guru himself served food to the *sangat*.

In his time, Baba Sri Chand, the elder son of Guru Nanak, founded the sect of *Udasi*s with deep ascetic traditions

Guru Angad

64

of the old Hindu order. But Guru Angad countered this threat vigorously, calling them *Manmukh* or self-centred. He established as many as 131 new *sangat*s.

In due time Guru Angad selected Guru Amar Das as his successor just as Nanak had selected him.

An interesting but seemingly a true incident finally clinched the selection of next Guruship for Amar Das. The story goes like this: One night, it was raining heavily. Well before dawn, Amar Das was returning from the river with the brass utensil full of water when he slipped and fell near a weaver's frame. Hearing the unusual thud, the weaver asked his wife, "Who could there be at this unearthly hour?" She said, "Who else could he be than Amru *Nathawan* (a word of great derision meaning someone perfectly shelterless)?" Amar Das, however, heard this insult with amusement. Next day, when the Guru held his court, he asked Amar Das if any incident had taken place while bringing the water. Amar Das though embarrassed, could not tell a lie. He repeated what had happened.

At that time, what the Guru said is now a part of the Sikh prayer. It says, "O Amar Das, you shall be a shelter for the shelterless; honour for those without honour; provider for those without succour; patron for those without a patron." At the end, the Guru said, "*tu sab ka swami*" (You will be the master of all.)

Guru Angad also ignored the claims of his sons to exalt Amar Das as the next Sikh Guru. The new Guru was then seventy-three years old. He remained on Nanak's throne for more than 22 years.

Guru Amar Das's reign (1552 AD to 1574 AD) is quite eventful in the development of Sikhism. He was an untiring organizer and a zealous social reformer. He immersed himself wholly in the *Nam*.

Guru Amar Das

He held great religious debates with *Jogi*s, ascetics and *sanyasi*s of every description. Some of the more noted debates were held when he had undertaken pilgrimages to Kurukshetra and Hardwar. These pilgrimages have an important historical context.

It is well known that after his meeting with the Guru, in 1571 at his headquarters at Goindwal, emperor Akbar abolished the pilgrim tax on the Hindus and persuaded him to undertake a pilgrimage to Hardwar. The emperor also abolished the hated *jazia* only two years later, and also gifted a piece of land to Bhani, the daughter of Guru Amar Das, on which was later constructed the city of Amritsar by the fourth Guru Ram Das, her husband. Such was the Guru's impression on the Emperor.

During Guru Amar Das's time, the Sikh *sangat*s, now spread all over India, were organized in 22 *manjis*

Akbar, the Great, is seen here sitting in the *Pangat* to partake of the Guru's langar, before having an audience with Guru Amardas, the third Sikh Lord.

(bishoprics) and 52 *pirrha*s (parishes). Not just that, collectors known as *Masand*s were appointed to put the finances on sound footing. In addition, many elaborate rituals were simplified and some repugnant social customs, persecuting women like *sati* and *purdah* were abolished. But more importantly, an 84-step well or staired *Baoli* was constructed at Goindwal, which substituted the Ganga in the eyes of the common Sikhs. Like the Ganga, it was supposed to be capable of conferring salvation. Thus, during his reign, the Sikhs started asserting their identity independent of the Hindus.

The third Nanak was also a good poet. He composed poetry in simple language and easily understood metaphor. His famous composition *Anand* (joy) consisting of 40 verses finds an exalted place in the Guru Granth. It is this composition which, in its abbreviated form, is recited at all the Sikh ceremonies.

Now, let us see how Guru Amar Das discovered his successor. Jetha was born on September 24, 1534 in a Sodhi family of Lahore. He lost his parents when still very young. So, he came to live in a village named Bisarke, with his grandmother. At that time, Amar Das at the behest of Guru Angad, too was camping in that village.

Being very poor, Jetha used to sell gram in the village. He would sell gram in and around the Guru's hermitage as well and listen to the discourses of Amar Das. Since, he was a lad of very striking presence, Amar Das noticed him and when he moved back to Goindwal, Jetha felt like accompanying him.

When Guru Amar Das' younger daughter Bhani became marriageable, the third Guru selected Jetha as her bridegroom. This marriage is a very important event in the history of Sikh church. Guru Amar Das ignored the claim to succession of his two sons and the elder son-in-law when selecting Ram Das as the fourth Guru.

Hazrat Mian Mir, a Muslim Sufi with his disciples. Mian Mir twice played a very conspicious role in strengthening the Sikh Church.

Guru Ram Das (1574 AD to 1581 AD) was 40 when he became the fourth Nanak. However, it is during his Guruship that the Sikh church assumed a more concrete shape.

He was yet to be nominated as Guru when Ram Das began to develop a township on the land that Akbar had gifted to his wife. Some additional land was also purchased for this purpose. This settlement was named as *Guru ka Chak*. It had an ancient pool that was considered very holy. Guru Ram Das sufficiently enlarged it and named it Ramsar or the pool of Rama.

It is this township which since the time of the fifth Nanak has come to be known as Amritsar. In due course, the headquarters of the Sikh church were shifted to the new township. It is remarkable that the young Sikh movement was resourceful enough to build such a major and strategic township. For, overtime it became the commercial capital of Punjab.

Guru Ram Das was a poetic genius. He composed a number of new *Raga*s or musical metres. The Guru Granth contains 638 of his hymns. But of particular interest are the four hymns known as *Lavan* (the circumambulatory verses) that form the fulcrum of the Sikh wedding ceremony known as *Anand Karaj* or the ceremony of joy.

He also prescribed a daily code of conduct whose worship for the Sikhs was distinct from the Hindus. However, it was on the question of succession that the Sikh church took a major new turn. The story goes like this: One day Guru Ram Das sat on a low chair called *pirhi* for his prayers. Bibi Bhani saw that one leg of that chair could give way. So, she placed her palm below that weakened leg. For as long as the Guru remained in meditation, Bhani bore the pain so much so that her palm started bleeding. When the Guru rose from his *samadhi*, he found blood on the floor. Thus, Bibi Bhani, his wife, won a boon from the

Guru Ram Das

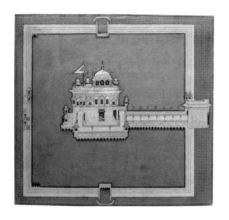

A vision-model of the holy Darbar Sahib in middle of the Pool of Nectar.

fourth Guru that hereafter the Guruship would belong to the progeny only. In other words, all Gurus hereafter would be her linear descendents.

Bibi Bhani and Guru Ram Das had three sons, Prithvi Chandra, Mahadev and Arjan. The eldest son, Prithvi, had fallen from father's grace as he had shown symptoms of greed and ambition during the construction of Amritsar. The second son, Mahadev, was almost a recluse with no interest in the world. So, the choice was Arjan, the youngest son who appeared fully qualified to assume the Guruship of the Sikh movement. Arjan was installed as the fifth Nanak in 1581 at the age of 18 years. He remained at the helm of affairs for the next 25 years.

The reign of **Guru Arjan (1581 AD to 1606 AD)** is really epochmaking in the annals of Sikh church. It is during his tenure that Guru Granth Sahib or the *Adi* Granth as it was then called, was put together and installed in the Harmandir Sahib (Golden Temple), the temple constructed at the centre of the 'pool of nectar' in Amritsar. It is this event that made the Sikh movement a full-fledged religion which means having all the three ingredients of an organized religion viz. a messiah, a book and a centralized church. A very significant aspect of this development is that it made the Sikhs also the 'People of the Book', (which Islam is not ordained to persecute) so that the people of the book could not be classed as infidels.

Guru Arjan was a great builder. Apart from completing the construction of Amritsar, he founded three new towns. These are: Gobindpur, now known as Hargobindpur on the right bank of the Beas, Taran Taran, 23 kms south of Amritsar and Kartarpur, 15 kms north-west of Jalandhar.

But his greatest architectural achievement shall remain the construction of Harmandir Sahib, the foundation stone of which was laid by the famous Sufi saint Hazrat Mian Mir in 1588. A most outstanding feature of this architecture is that it combines the Hindu temple and the Muslim mosque. Hence it is of a piece with Nanak's first statement *'Na Koi Hindu; Na Mussalman.'*

Putting together the *Adi* Granth, the Sikh Bible, required enormous literary talents, indefatigable zeal, immense patience, matchless editorial skill and enough time and energy, all at one's command. They say that the *Mool Mantra* and the *Japuji* were written by Guru Arjan himself. Thereafter, he dictated the entire body of the *Adi* Granth to Bhai Gurdas. It consists of 5751 *shabad*s or hymns of which 4829 are by the first five Gurus including Arjan himself and 789 by the *Bhakta*s. The Guru in the tradition of Nanak too was a matchless poet. His masterpiece *'Sukhmani Sahib'* makes a large part of the Granth.

Guru Arjan

Guru Arjan dictating the Guru Granth to Bhai Gurdas.

This *Adi* Granth was ceremoniously installed in the Harmandir Sahib in 1604. Now, this great event divides the Sikh movement into two equal halves. It completes the *Bhakti* or the pacifist mode of Sikhism, after which, the *Shakti* or the militant mode takes over. And between these two phases lies the watershed martyrdom of Guru Arjan himself.

Jehangir, the new Moghul emperor, was not one known for religious tolerance. In addition, he harboured a grievance against Guru Arjan that his rebellious son Khusrau had received his support. However, the *Tuzzuk-e-Jehangiri* or the personal diary of Jehangir tells us rather clearly that he had long made up his mind to put an end to the Sikh movement. The Guru was therefore summoned to Lahore in 1606 and ordered to be put to death with utmost cruelty. The alternative offered to him was that to save his life he would have to embrace Islam. The Guru spurned the offer. The traditional Sikh accounts mention that Guru Arjan was made to sit on a hot iron plate and burning hot sand was poured over his body.

The Guru earned his martyrdom on May 13, 1606, within seven months of Akbar's death. This was the first major martyrdom among the Sikhs.

Guru Arjan, opted for a torturous death over embracing Islam.

However, Guru Arjan's parting advice to his son and successor Guru Hargobind was that the Sikhs should hereafter arm themselves in self-defence. This was a logical development of the teachings of Nanak. However, the Sikhs taking to arms was a hugely qualitative change too.

The Martial Mode (1606 AD to 1675 AD)

Guru Hargobind

Guru Hargobind (1606 AD to 1644 AD), the sixth Nanak, was only 11 when he succeeded Guru Arjan. However, his anointing as the next Guru by Baba Buddha, is a highly inspiring story in itself that has a large bearing on the growth of later Sikhism.

When Baba Buddha was about to put Guru Hargobind formally on the seat of Guruship, the young Guru said, "Babaji, have you forgotten father's martyrdom? Now, we also need to acquire the additional knowledge of arms." Accordingly, Baba Buddha put a sword on his right side instead of the left. It is said that when the venerable Baba tried to correct his mistake as the sword of *Miri* (temporal affairs) should have been put on the left side, the young Guru very precociously said to him, "Babaji, let it remain like this only. This sword of *Miri* will now onwards be the sword of compassion."

The new Guru asked the Sikhs to henceforth start dealing in horses and presenting weapons to him. What it meant was that the Sikhs were now to lay equal emphasis on developing physical as well as spiritual faculties. Hereafter, *Tegh* (the sword) and *Degh* (the community kitchen) were to go hand in hand with victory (*Fateh*). The Jats, the rough and ready soldiers of the Panth, now joined the Sikh movements in huge numbers.

In 1608, Guru Hargobind laid the foundation of the Akal Takht or the 'Throne of the Immortal' in front of the Harmandir. Now it was to be the Guru's seat of temporal power. Sitting there, he would watch wrestling bouts and the feats of swordmanship of his disciples. Not just that, he had also begun to dispense justice from there. Now the Sikh church was 'a state within a state'.

In 1609, Guru Hargobind laid the foundation of the fort of Lohgarh to house soldiers and war-horses. This fort was completed in 1612. He also built a rampart around the city of Amritsar. They say, the Guru created a fighting force of 5000-strong and maintained a well-trained posse of his personal bodyguards.

The Moghul Governor of Punjab now started sending alarming reports to Jehangir about the war-like preparations of the Guru. A Hindu courtier also wanted the Guru to be punished and was carrying sinister tales to the court to add fuel to the fire. So, the Guru was duly summoned to Delhi. But when he reached there, he was arrested and sent to the Gwalior fort. The Guru was then hardly 18 years' old. It was well known that those sent to Gwalior seldom returned alive.

The Guru remained incarcerated in the Gwalior fort for almost seven years. The Sikhs then waited upon the old Hazrat Mian Mir and sought his intercession. The Hazrat was particularly sad at the way his friend Guru Arjan had been martyred. However, he was also now the spiritual mentor of Jehangir's fond queen, Nur Jehan.

Thus, Jehangir ordered the release of Guru Hargobind. The Guru refused to be released alone. He asked the emperor to release all the other 52 princes, who were undergoing imprisonment in Gwalior. At last, the Guru's wish was granted. This great act of compassion earned the Guru the epithet of 'Bandi Chor', the one who got the prisoners released.

Guru Hargobind, thereafter, devoted much time and energy to strengthen his forces. Now Jehangir too did not seem to have any objection to the Guru strengthening his militia or maintaining personal bodyguards. Soon, the Guru was involved in an armed clash with his Hindu distracter Chandu whose relatives had occupied Gobindpur. This led to two skirmishes within days of each other. However, the Guru emerged victorious in both. There two battles marked the course of things to come.

The Akal Takht, the seat of Guru's temporal power.

71

Meanwhile, one of the princes who had earned his freedom from the Gwalior fort because of Guru Hargobind called upon him to offer him a piece of land in the Shivalik hills. The Guru established the town of Kiratpur on that land so that he could take shelter there in the event of an emergency.

In 1634, the Guru had to face the Moghuls. This battle was fought at the village of Jhabal. It continued for nine hours, in which the Moghul commander was killed and Moghul forces had to beat a retreat. The second battle was fought when Painda Khan, a foster brother of the Guru, joined hands with the Moghuls. This battle took place in 1635 in which the Guru killed Painda Khan in a duel. Soon enough, another skirmish took place in which enough blood was shed. It was after this skirmish that the Guru retired to the safety of Kiratpur in the Shivalik hills.

A significant event is the Sixth Guru's chance encounter with the Maratha Saint, *Samarath* Guru Ram Das at Sri Nagar (Garhwal). The Maratha Guru was surprised to see the Sikh Guru in full regalia, riding the horse and donning two swords. The Maratha Guru asked the Sikh Guru,. "What kind of hermit are you?" He replied, "Internally a hermit and externally a prince." This, they say, inspired the Maratha Guru in initiating his ward, Shivaji to the life of national upliftment.

After 1640, the Guru started losing his interest in his princely ways and was turning inwards. So, he selected Har Rai, the second son of Baba Gurditta, as the seventh Nanak at the young age of 14 years.

Guru Har Rai (1644 AD to 1661), the seventh Nanak, was by nature a pacifist. However, he took several steps to consolidate the Sikh movement from his headquarters at Kiratpur. A large number of new recruits embraced Sikhism and leading families of the area joined the Sikh movement.

The new Guru, continued to maintain the regal style of his grandfather and duly kept armed retainers. He had good relations with Shah Jehan particularly after he was instrumental in sending some medicinal herbs that had promoted the recovery of Dara Shikoh, the emperor's favourite son, from some serious illness.

However, it was during his reign that Aurangzeb came to occupy the throne of Delhi and aimed at exercising some control on the Sikh movement. The charge against Guru Har Rai was twofold: One, that in the war of succession, he had given some help to Dara Shikoh; and two, that the Guru Granth Sahib contained some remarks derogatory to Islam. Thus, the Guru was summoned to the imperial court.

Guru Har Rai

However, it goes to the credit of Guru Har Rai that he wrote back to the Emperor the following missive:

> "It is against the principles and traditions of the Sikh Gurus to go to any king's court either for any favour or for political submission … I do not deny Dara Shikoh who came here and met me a number of times, was my friend … I blessed Dara Shikoh with the spiritual kingdom of God.

> "Since Your Majesty has expressed such a keen interest in gaining knowledge about the faith of Baba Nanak and the mysteries of our scriptures, I am sending my elder son Ram Rai along with some Sikh missionaries to remove your doubts and misgivings about the Sikh religion."

Not just that, the Guru also instructed his son to fearlessly interpret the Sikh scriptures and the history of the great Gurus. He was also told that he carried with him the blessings of Guru Nanak. This was all befitting the house of Nanak.

In Islam, a holy man is one who can perform some miracles (*Karamat*). Ram Rai was able to satisfy the court on this account. But he was unable to take the rightful stand regarding the reference to Mussalmans. When the Guru learnt what had transpired, he was very angry. He admonished his son and asked him never to show him his face again.

Thereupon, Ram Rai started opposing his father, claiming the Guruship for himself, at the instigation of Aurangzeb. But both the Sikh *sangat* and the Guru rejected his claim. The Guru died at the very young age of 31. It is believed that Aurangzeb, with the connivance of Ram Rai, had been able to administer poison to him.

But before the Guru left for his heavenly journey, he passed on the Nanakship to his younger son Har Kishan who became the eighth Nanak at the tender age of five years. But this made the Sikhs very happy nonetheless as they could not countenance the prospect of Ram Rai ascending the throne of the Guru.

Guru Har Kishan (1661 to 1664), the Eighth Nanak, was so full of the grace of Nanakhood that everything started getting accomplished almost automatically. The Sikh lore has it that he displayed unusual maturity and impressed the *sangat* even with his discourses. But the Ram Rai camp was disaffected. Ultimately, Ram Rai himself went to Delhi to press for his claim.

Aurangzeb wanted nothing better than this to happen. Ultimately, he decided to summon the young Guru to his court. The job of bringing the child Guru from Kiratpur to Delhi was entrusted to Mirza Raja Jai Singh of Jaipur who was a very trusted general and grandee of the court.

Guru Har Kishan

However, he made the emperor to solemnly swear that no harm whatsoever would come to the person of the Guru. Jai Singh in turn entrusted the job to his trusted Dewan with the instructions that he should do the needful with utmost tact and humility.

When the Sikhs came to know of Aurangzeb's summons, they were greatly perturbed. But the Dewan told them that as long as Raja Jai Singh was alive, he would not let any harm come to *Guruji*. Finally, the Guru's party including his mother escorted by the Rajputs, started for Delhi. After some time they camped at Panjokhra, a village near Ambala. It was here that a miracle took place.

A certain learned Brahmin of the village challenged the Guru to interpret the Gita. The Guru in all humility asked the Pandit to bring anyone from the village to have the Gita interpreted. So, he brought a rank illiterate *jheevar*, a lowly water carrier, to the Guru. Guru Harkishan looked into the eyes of the *jheevar* who instantly felt illuminated and began to give a wonderful exposition of the verses he was asked to interpret. Upon that, the Pandit immediately embraced the Nanak Panth.

The Guru was accommodated in the palace of Raja Jai Singh at Raisina. It is here that the Gurdwara of Bangla Sahib stands today.

As soon as the Guru reached Delhi, a cholera epidemic broke out. The Guru gave to each one suffering a sip of his *charanamrit* (the nectar of his feet) and cured them all.

However, after some time, small pox too appeared in epidemic form. The Guru shifted his camp to the banks of the Jamuna. The Guru had a choice to go to Aurangzeb's court but he didn't. He was not spared from the epidemic either. So he promptly appointed his successor without the consent of the Moghul court.

The devout however believe that this was the way the house of Nanak defeated the nefarious designs of Aurangzeb. The reigning Sikh Guru was at no cost going to present himself in the court of any king, much less that of the wily Aurangzeb.

Guru Tegh Bahadur (1665 to 1675), the ninth Nanak, was the grand uncle of Guru Har Kishan. He lived at Baba Bakala ever since the death of his father Guru Har Gobind in 1644. In his youth, he had greatly distinguished himself as a swordsman and that gave him his popular name as the 'warrior of the sword'. However, now he spent most of his time in meditation.

As soon as the eighth Nanak said that the Guru was at Baba Bakala, several claimants and imposters (22 is the number mentioned) came to Baba Bakala and established their *Manjis* or seats there. So, the question now was how to find out the true Guru.

Guru Tegh Bahadur

Meanwhile, a certain rich Sikh merchant named Makkhan Shah Lubana came to Baba Bakala in search of the true Guru. His problem was that his ship, full of costly merchandise, had got caught in a storm on the high seas. He had, therefore, prayed to the Guru that if the ship survived the lashing of the waves and everything went well, he would make an offering of 100 gold coins to him. He now had to redeem his obligation. But what was he to do? A score of Gurus were there and all of them made equally tall claims. So, he devised a stratagem.

He decided to give one gold coin to each Guru. Finally when his attention was brought to a certain Guru who was living like a recluse, he went up to him and placed the coin as an offering before him. But the Guru said, 'O my dear disciple! You owe me much more. Where is the rest of the money? Needless to say, Lubana had found the true Guru.

Gurdwara Rakab Gunj.

But the assumption of Guruship by Guru Tegh Bahadur without reference to the Moghul court annoyed Aurangzeb so much so that he ordered his arrest. The Guru with his entourage was at Damdhan when he was taken into custody in the end of 1665.

The story has it that Aurangzeb wanted the Guru to show him *Karamat* (miracle) consistent with his spiritual position or be ready to die. The Guru refused the first option and accepted the second one. They say that Aurangzeb had actually ordered the death of the Guru but the punishment was commuted at the intercession of Raja Ram Singh, the son of none other than Mirza Raja Jai Singh. It was after more than a month's detention that the Guru and his party were released.

Thereafter, the Guru proceeded eastwards and left his family at Patna. At that time, Mata Gujri gave birth to her son Gobind Rai. However, at that time, the Ninth Nanak was on missionary tours to eastern Uttar Pradesh and Bihar with occasional visits to Orissa and Bengal. That, they say, explains why his message of Sikhism is couched in extremely simple language. He also visited many older Sikh *sangat*s like those of Dacca and Chittagong, established from the days of Nanak.

Gurdwar Bangla Sahib.

At the invitation of Raja Ram Singh, he also went to Assam and spent about two years there. It is said that the Guru was also instrumental in saving the Raja of Assam from the wrath of Aurangzeb and then marked the limits respectively of the Moghuls and the kingdom of Assam. When he returned to Patna from his missionary activity in Bengal and Assam, his son Gobind Rai was already four years old. Now he decided to head back home, sending his family with some members of his Darbar. They reached Lakhnaur near Ambala in September 1670. He himself, however, took a circuitous route to reach Lakhnaur.

75

Kashmiri Pandits explaining to Guru Tegh Bahadur how Aurangzeb was intent upon converting them into Muslims.

It is that time in the history of India when Aurangzeb decided to reverse the policy of religious tolerance of his great grandfather Akbar. In 1669, he had ordered the closure of non-Muslim schools and demolition of places of Hindu worship in order to build mosques on their sites. Not only that, he now launched upon religious conversion of the Hindus with vengeance with the declared aim of converting the land from *Daral Harab* to *Daral Islam*. However, a large number of Hindus embraced Sikhism at the call of the Guru.

When in 1675, the Guru returned from his missionary tours across Punjab, he received a deputation of the Kashmiri Pandits who had come to wait upon him. They wanted him to guide them as to what they should do to escape forcible conversion. The Guru observed that the occasion demanded some noble soul to make supreme sacrifice in order to shame the bigoted emperor.

At that time, the young Gobind Rai just playfully entered the court and is reported to have said, "Who is nobler than you, O father?" Thus, the die was cast, for, the Guru then told the Kashmiri Pandits to convey to the emperor that if Guru Tegh Bahadur got converted, they would follow suit. This is perhaps the only example of its kind in the history of mankind when some great divine chose to embrace martyrdom for saving the faith of those that did not strictly belong to his fold. Thus, the house of Nanak helped charter absolutely a new course in human history.

Apprehending summons from the royal court, the Guru nominated his young son as the next Nanak on July 8, 1675 and accompanied by five of his followers, set out for Delhi. The Nawab of Sirhind had already received royal orders for the arrest of the Guru. So, they were detained at Bassi Pathan and kept there for three months. Here, they were offered all kinds of inducements and when these failed to work, they were tortured to force them to get converted. But when nothing worked, they were moved to Delhi for the enactment of the final drama.

Two of his companions, namely Bhai Mati Das and Bhai Diala were done to death with great torture before the very eyes of the Guru. Then the Guru was asked to show some *Karamat* (miracle) to escape the fate awaiting him. But the unbending stand of the Guru was that none should ever try to intervene in God's own scheme of things. The executioner severed the Guru's head with a single blow. The Gurdwara of Sisganj was built at the place where the Guru's head fell. And the Gurdwara Rakab Ganj stands where his body was cremated. Both make Delhi's adorning structures today.

Guru Tegh Bahadur refusing to perform any miracles, relenting to God's own scheme of things, unafraid of his executioners. After his martyrdom, the ninth Guru came to the known as *"Hind ki Chadar"* meaning the sheet that covers the honour of *Dharma* in India.

A painting of Guru Gobind
Singh (1675-1708) This painting
symbolically potrays the Guru
having reached the end of the earth,
keeping his 'chin up', the essential
meaning of *Chardi Kala*.

An Extraordinary Transformation   Chapter VIII

Gobind Rai or **Gobind Das (later, Gobind Singh)** (1675 to 1708) was hardly nine years-old when he became the tenth Nanak. It is believed that a Muslim divine in the village of Karnal looked at the sky at the time of his birth and bowed towards the East — something against the injunctions of Islam. When asked, his answer was, "There is a soul born in the East today, who will re-establish the rule of law (*Dharma*) in the land."

The story further says that the divine then travelled to Patna to have the sight of the newborn in person. And when he saw him, he held two *handi*s (clay vessels), one full of milk and the other full of water. The infant touched both the vessels. Those assembled were intrigued by it and asked its significance. He replied that in touching both the vessels the child had indicated that he would be impartial towards both the Muslims and the Hindus.

But the real significance of Guru Gobind Singh is that he, as the tenth Nanak, crowned the full range of achievements of all the nine Nanaks before him. He also created in the form of Sikhism the first corporate religion of the world in which Nanak is an immanent experience to every Sikh in the form of 'Shabad Guru' that means the Guru Granth as the living Nanak. He was a multi-faceted genius.

From the *Japuji* to the Jap Sahib

Guru Gobind Singh's super-humanness can be judged from the fact that when he could not get the official copy of the Guru Granth Sahib, he dictated it from his memory alone.

The need to dictate the Guru Granth Sahib afresh was, becoming very pressing for him. Perhaps he had already decided to create the '**Nam**' in form of Guru Granth. His mind, it seems, was made up to end Nanak's personal Guruship among the Sikhs.

Nanak aimed at creating a new Man out of an utterly lifeless society. And, its culmination came when the tenth Nanak created the Khalsa (defenders of the *Dharma*) or the men with five K's in his own image. This man of *Karma* and *Dharma* is, in essence, the same as the *Sachiara* of Nanak who hates none and fears none. The jingle of pen pictures that the tenth Nanak has created in his martial poetry, can indeed transform the weak and timid into ones ever-prepared to beard lions in their own dens, Banda Singh Bahadur is a shining sample of which.

The Resplendent Drama

As an inspired poet and literary genius, the tenth Nanak accomplished something extraordinary. Apart

Guru Gobind Singh is seen here exhorting *Bairagi* Madho Das to leave his path of resignation and come back to the path of commitment.

79

from his autobiographical work, '*Vichitra Natak*' or the 'Resplendent Drama', he also gave new interpretations to such eventful lives as those of Lord Rama and Lord Krishna in his '*Ramavatar*' and '*Krishnavtar*', respectively. The sum and substance of this new interpretation is that the sword remains the last arbiter of the conflict between *Dharma* and *Adharma* — the battle these heroes fought relentlessly as their life's mission. Some scholars of Sikh divinity, however, do not consider portions of the "Resplendent Drama" as authentic, as they feel that these seem to clash with Nanak's basic thought structure.

In fact, nothing fascinated the Guru more than the clashing of steel in bloody battles. That's why, he gave God a new name. This new name of God is '*Sarbaloh*' which means all steel. But even so, his quintessential message remains that of Nanak only. Besides, he had most of the popular religious literature of the Hindus translated into the *Brajbhasha*, the main medium of self-expression in those days. His court they say was adorned by as many as 52 poets. Unfortunately, most of the literature created by him or in his court at his instance, was washed away in the floods of the *Sirsa* rivulet when he was retreating from Anandpur.

Birth of the Khalsa

Now, let us try to repeat the story of the birth of Khalsa though no language can really re-enact the drama that took place at Anandpur Sahib on the *Baisakhi* day of 1699. The tenth Nanak had prepared himself for 20 long years for such a moment of destiny. It was a tumultuous affair — an annual congregation of thousands of Sikhs that had come to pay homage to their Guru. All of a sudden, he drew his sword, flashed it and cried out, "Is there any Sikh who is prepared to offer his head to me?"

A complete hush fell over the benumbed assembly. No one came forward. The following words were recollected as exhortiation of the first Nanak "If you are fond of playing the game of love with me, then come to me, placing your head on the palm of your hand," One Sikh stood up and came forward to offer his head to the Guru. The Guru took him behind a screen. The assembly heard the blade of the Guru's sword slicing through body and bone. The Guru emerged from behind the screen, blood dripping from his bloody sword and repeated his call.

By that time, the mood had stabilized. Thus, came forward another Sikh to offer his head. In this manner, five times did the Guru call and apparently five Sikhs were beheaded behind the screen. But then, like a master magician, he brought them all back in new clothes with smiles on their lips. This is how the Sikh lore records the birth of the Khalsa.

Guru Gobind Singh, getting ready to administer *'Khande Bate da Amrit'* to *Panj Piare* or the Five Beloved, after the birth of the Khalsa.

"Himself the Guru; Himself the Disciple"

The five men he had beheaded, four of whom belonged to the lower castes, were by virtue of passing through that baptismal of fire, exalted to the status of *'Panj Piare'* or the Beloved Five. It is this assembly of the five that heads the Khalsa Panth. This is the highest body of the Khalsa. But perhaps the importance of this baptismal lies elsewhere. Soon after, the Guru begged to the exalted five to administer the same baptismal to him. And when it was done, the Guru was also renamed from Gobind Das to Gobind Singh.

Another example of this corporate religion comes from the battle of Chamkaur. In that battle, the odds weighed heavily against the Sikhs and there was every danger that even the Guru could meet his end. At that time, the Five of the Khalsa collectively asked the Guru to leave the field of action so that even if the battle was lost, the war could continue in the hope of the ultimate victory. The Guru was adamant. But before this august assembly of the five or the *'Panj Piare'*, he could not but bow. This, in effect, is the first *Hukamnama* or ordinance of the corporate Sikh Church.

81

Creating the First and only Corporate Religion of the World

The real touch of the Guru was given to the corporate religion a little before the Tenth Nanak breathed his last. The Nanakhood that had gone on uninterrupted for almost 240 years appeared destined to end with the death of Tenth Lord. For, there was none left in the lineage of the Guru who could be the claimant of next Nanakhood as all the four *Sahibzada*s (sons) had embraced martyrdom in his very lifetime. Now, who would be the Guru? At that time, the Guru passed on his Nanakhood to the Sri Guru Granth Sahib as the Word Guru. Thus, Sri Guru Granth Sahib received the unique distinction of becoming the body of the living Nanak. In other words, with this act, Nanakhood became eternal in the form of the 'Guru Granth'. It means that all the ten Nanaks became immanent in the body of the Granth. Thus, every baptised Sikh of the Guru lives in the immanence of the Guru each moment of his life. There is not a moment in the life of a Sikh when he is alone and bereft of the grace of the Guru, flowing on to him.

An Unrivalled Leader of Men and a Peerless Military Genius

Guru Gobind Singh was an unrivalled leader and organizer of men as also an equally peerless military genius. The Khalsa he created as a rough and ready soldier of *Dharma* and *Karma* made sparrows face fierce falcons in actual battles. The Sikh slogan of '*Chardi Kala*' which means to always keep the chin up even while facing the worst, gains its true significance from the *Zafar Namah* or 'Epistle of Victory' that the Guru wrote to the Emperor.

*Sant Sepahi*s and the *Dharma Yuddha*

The new uniform of the Khalsa had deep roots in tradition. But such was the enduring basis of this transformation — fighting the tyrant rulers as *Dharma Yuddha* — that none whatsoever backed out. The oceanic nursery of *Sehajdhari* Sikhs in particular and the Hindus of Punjab in general, swearing by the religion of Nanak, stood rock-like behind the Guru's *Sant Sepahi*s and just did not allow the flame of revolution to die out. Not one cared to know when Guru Nanak's power of the **Nam** changed into power of the sword of Guru Gobind Singh. Thus, this transition appeared just in order.

The Famous Oration

Here is a summary of the famous oration of the tenth Guru to the assembly of the *Baisakhi* of 1699 at Anandpur (in which the order of the Khalsa took birth):

"From now on you have become casteless. No ritual, either Hindu or Muslim, shall you perform. You shall believe in no superstition. You shall believe only in one God, the Master who is the only Creator and Destroyer. In your new order, each shall to the other be a brother. You shall lead the life of a pure householder but sacrifice it all at the call of *Dharma*. Women shall be equal of their men in every way. They shall observe no *Purdah* (veil) nor shall the widows be burnt alive on the pyres of their dead husbands. Besides, he who kills his own daughter, the Khalsa shall not have anything to do with him. Every Sikh male shall hereafter end his name with the word Singh (lion) and every woman with Kaur (princess). You shall forsake smoking, meat done in the Muslim way and unsuitable contact with a Muslim woman."

This oration also fixed the Khalsa uniform: the five K's of the Khalsa identity. These are: (1) the *Keshas* or the unshorn hair like those of the old sages and warriors; (2) the *Kangha* or the comb to keep the hair clean and well-combed; (3) the *Kara* or the steel bangle or bracelet which has several meanings some of which even esoteric but which in the main is to protect the hand that weilds the sword; (4) the *Kirpan* or the sword for self defence and fighting the righteous battle; and (5) the *Kacchha* or the innerwear which also symbolises a life of chastity. Not just that, a householder with one wife was to be considered a chaste man. The unshorn hair was to be tied in a bun on which the Guru ordained the Sikhs to tie a turban. They were also ordained to greet each other with '*Waheguruji ka Khalsa; Waheguruji Ki Fateh*' which means 'The Khalsa belongs to God and victory belongs to Him.' This, in essence, meant that victory belonged to the Khalsa.

In the same baptismal, Guru Gobind Singh conferred upon the Khalsa five negations or in other words, five freedoms born of these negations. This is the concept of his *Nash* or doctrine. In short, these five negations are:

1. *Dharma Nash* which means no *Dharma* shall hereafter bind you. While no one can live meaningfully without *Dharma*, here it seems to free the man of the duties and obligations born of the cause and effect of the inexorable cycle of births and deaths.

2. *Bhrama Nash* which means the complete destruction of superstitions, complexes and inhibitions. Rousseau, the philosopher of the French Revolution perhaps aimed at just this kind of freedom when he said, "Man was born free but is in chains everywhere." It is like rejecting all the constraints of civilization.

3. *Kul Nash* which means you shall no longer belong to your father and mother or the family lineage. In fact, the Khalsa baptismal makes one so baptized as the son of Guru Gobind Singh and Mata Sahib Dewan only. That is the reason why Banda Singh Bahadur after becoming a Khalsa, adopted the surname of Sodhi — the family caste of Guru

Keshas

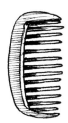

Kangha

Kara

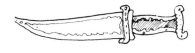

Kirpan

Kacchha

The uniform of the Khalsa identity consisting of the five **K**'s.

Gobind Singh. His children are known not by his Rajput lineage but as Sodhis.

4. *Karma Nash* which means that hereafter you have transcended the bondage of all *Karma* that keeps one in the cycle of births and deaths. Now no one can be free of this bondage as none can live without performing *Karma*. Hence, it means unattached action whereby the action is performed on behalf of the Guru or God only.

5. *Krit Nash* which means you are hereafter released from the bondage of earning the livelihood through trades and professions.

Thus, a Khalsa is nearest to what a *Nihang* is — the one whom neither victory nor defeat, neither success nor failure, neither happiness nor grief, neither love nor hatred, neither gold nor dust, neither enemity nor friendship and neither appreciation nor rejection mean a thing.

The 40 *Mukta*s

The saga of how 40 Sikhs denounced the Guru in a formal disclaimer in the battle of Chamkaur but rejoined him in time for the battle of Rohi is quite unique in religious history. They chose to die fighting since there was no escape from death. This makes a fine example of the

Guru Gobind Singh tearing off the letter of denunciation by the 40 *Mukta*s in the battle at Muktsar. It is this letter that is known as '*Bedawa*'. The Gurdwara at Muktsar commemorates this poignant event.

84

A scene from one of Guru Gobind Singh's defensive battles.

new spirit the Guru had infused in the Sikhs. The story runs like this: 40 Sikhs deserted their Guru during battle and reached the safety of their homes. However, they were put to such extreme shame by their own women that they dressed for battle again. One woman Mata Bhag Kaur led them back to the Guru. She was injured in action but braved the fight. As for the 40 men, they fought too but were injured seriously.

The last wish of their leader Mahan Singh was that the Guru should pardon them before death claimed them. Strangely enough, the Guru had kept that letter of denunciation on his person like a heavy weight on his chest. Moved by the request, the Guru tore off that disclaimer before Mahan Singh actually died, naming those 40 Sikhs as 'Muktas' or the liberated ones. This episode took place where the Gurdwara of Muktsar (pool of the liberated souls) stands today. The town of Muktsar is named after them.

Defensive Battles Only

The battles that the Guru had to fight after creating the Khalsa cannot really be described in words as these were the ultimate tests of faith and human endurance. The Guru once had to stem the advancing tide of the Moghul army with only one Sikh who was sent to stall them. Not only

Pir Buddhu Shah of Sadhaura, a great admirer of the Guru, is seen offering the services of all his four sons to him, as in his eyes the Guru was fighting for righteousness that had to be defended by all without any distinction of caste and creed. It is a most shining example of its kind when the Muslims themselves came forward to lay down their lives to defend the Guru's cause.

that, he also sacrificed two of his sons in this fight. In fact, after the creation of Khalsa, the Guru got very little time to prepare for the battles to come. Hill chief of the surrounding kingdoms had become insecure and so attacked the fort of Anandpur almost within a year of that great event. Their main fear was that until the Guru was suppressed, their own caste privileges could be in danger. They therefore dislodged the Guru through a stratagem, but without luck. The Guru was back in Anandpur soon enough.

The real battle however started in 1705 when the Moghuls and the hill chiefs joined hands. This seige continued for almost seven months. The Guru finally vacated Anandpur but only after receiving solemn pledges of safe passage sworn on the holy Quran and in the name of the Emperor himself. But as soon as the Guru left the fort, pledges were thrown overboard and the Moghul forces went for the kill. These battles continued until the Guru reached wetlands (*bet*) of the Satluj in early 1706. Now the Guru was on a much safer and stronger ground. An estimate of how safe he felt, can be understood from the fact that on the *Baisakhi* day of 1706, he administered the baptismal of the Khalsa to 1,25,000 Sikhs.

Another important point: In the 18 battles fought between the period of the sixth and tenth Guru, not even a yard of the enemy territory was annexed. It underlined the intention of the battles that was purely defensive in nature. The Gurus were truly spiritual in their reasons for wars that were forced upon them, and their only objective was self-defense. However, after the exit of the tenth Nanak from the scene, the reasons changed to gain political supremacy. Now the Khalsa or the corporate Sikhism would fight for their own rule and kingdom in Punjab.

The Nanak Vision

For all the major changes that Guru Gobind Singh ushered into the format of Nanak's gospel, he was very clear that he was merely elaborating upon the message of Guru Nanak only. For example, of the ideological unity of the ten Nanaks, he most emphatically said:

> "Nanak transformed into Angad and spread *Dharma* in the world. He was called Amar Das in the next transformation. When opportune time came for the boon, the Guru was called Ram Das. Only the saints knew it; the fools did not. Those who recognized them as one, successfully understood the spirirtual phenomenon. When Ram Das was merged in the Lord, the Guruship was bestowed on Arjan. When he left for the abode of the Lord, Hargobind was seated on the throne. When Hargobind left for the abode of the Lord, Har Rai was seated in his place. Har Kishan (the next Guru) was his son. And after him, Tegh Bahadur became the Guru."

Thus, he brought this unbroken chain of the Nanak's resurrections right up to him. Only humility demanded that he did not name himself as the tenth Nanak. The point is that in the Sikh lore, the sole point of reference is Guru Nanak only.

Now let us see how Guru Gobind Singh defines the Khalsa. In one of his *Swayya*s (metrical composition), he says as under:

> "He who constantly keeps his mind intent upon
>   ever awake, living light of the consciousness;
> He who never swerves from the thought of One God;
> He who is adorned with full faith in Him;
> And he who is wholly steeped in the love of the Lord,
> And even by mistake never puts his faith in fasting;
> Or worship of tombs, sepulchres or crematoriums,
> Caring not for pilgrimages, alms, charities,
>   penances and austerities;
> Or anything else but devotion to One God;
> And in whose heart and soul shines the Divine Light
>   of the full moon —
> He is known as the Khalsa — the purest of the pure."

And to repeat, there was no difference between the 'Sachiara' of Guru Nanak and the Khalsa of Guru Gobind Singh. So deeply woven were they in spirit.

88   The famous Golden Temple at Amritsar.

Nanak Becomes Eternal

With Guru Granth Sahib becoming the 'Word Guru', Sikhism took a major step forward. And this made Sikhism, as it were, a unique church religion, standing for all that is positive in man's spiritual life. In fact, the vast *Sadh Sangat* or the congregation of the saints as the Sikh congregation is known now lived in direct immanence of Nanak. No wonder, it produced heroes and martyrs of unbelievable character so much so that they created history at every step of their life. Any lesser movement would have succumbed to the religious persecution of the Moghuls who had developed tremendous fear of the Sikhs becoming the new rulers of their land.

An Archetypal Hero, Warrior and Martyr

The first hero of corporate Sikhism is evidently Banda Singh Bahadur, the *Bairagi* whom the Tenth Nanak had motivated to take up arms in defence of *Dharma*. Within two years of the final merging of his mentor Guru Gobind Singh, Banda had fully demonstrated that the imperial Moghul armies could actually be defeated in open battles by the Sikhs. The alacrity with which he marshalled his scanty resources and the swiftness with which he handled his ill-trained cavalry in the battles, is no less in skill than that of a consummate general.

Banda Singh achieved what a few dream and only a handful accomplish. With his own example, he set a seal on the things to come on a much wider spectrum.

Banda Singh Bahadur, the archetypal Sikh hero and martyr, who left an immortal imprint on Sikh history.

89

For example, at the very outset, he gave a new code of conduct to his soldiers in battle. According to this code: (1) They were not to plunder the civil population; (2) they were not to slay a coward or put obstacles in the way of a fugitive or a run-away; (3) they were never to commit adultery; (4) they were not to commit any theft; (5) they were not to be friends with adulterers and house-breakers; and finally (6) they were expected to give utmost respect to the enemy women whom they were to escort to safety and restore to their families. Now no military machine in the world could follow this kind of ethics in the battle. And it was in total contrast with the ethics as followed by the Moghuls. Yet, the Sikhs swore their loyalty to it.

It is remarkable that Banda Singh had established the first sovereign Sikh kingdom in Punjab almost in no time. He, therefore, assumed the title of Bahadur and not king. Not just that, in lieu of this sovereignty of the Khalsa, he also struck coins in the name of Nanak. The inscriptions on his seals and coins were later to be emulated by the future Sikh kings as well.

Another very important aspect of his military conquests is the honourable treatment that the mass of Muslims got from him. Thus, 500 Muslims had actually enlisted themselves in his army even when the *Jehad* was being invoked against him. These Muslim soldiers enjoyed full freedom of conscience to follow their own religion.

But the greatest act of his perhaps is that he gave the land back to the tillers, thus ending the exploitation of the real farmer by the privileged few. He thus established *Satyuga* or the rule of *Dharma* in his dominion, something totally unheard of in those times. And he went beyond himself by appointing the lower castes to offices of profit and influence in his government. In short, he gave a completely new orientation to the entire society.

William Irvine, a British historian, is on record having testified how the lower castes left their homes at his call and when they returned with their letters of appointments from him, the high-castes went all out to welcome them.

However, in 1716, as a result of a treacherous move by the Moghuls, Banda Singh found himself surrendering to them along with 700 of his soldiers. He was put in an iron cage and taken in a victory procession to Delhi. Some stragglers who had come to watch the spectacle, were also captured because they had maintained unshorn hair and were made to join procession. Thus, when the convoy reached Delhi after two months, the number of those accompanying him had actually swelled to 794.

They were all given one choice: either embrace Islam or die. Not one hesitated to give up his life. Banda Singh had to witness all their deaths and worse, the gory death of his young wife, and finally, that of his infant son who was tortured mercilessly before his eyes.

Banda Singh was spared no atrocity imaginable when it was his turn to die. He bore it stoically and heroically, thus shedding undying glory on the martyrology of the Sikh Panth. John Surnam and Edward Stephenson, the two British ambassadors, wrote thus from their personal testimony about this immortal saga: "It is not a little remarkable with what patience they undergo their fate, and to the last it has not been found that one apostatised from this new-found religion."

Other Sikh Martyrs

The next 50 years saw two *Ghallughara*s (mass killings) of the Sikhs. In fact, every Sikh had a price on his head. Every day at the *Nakha*s, the horse market of Lahore, hundreds met their end. But with each persecution they emerged stronger, so much so that in 1765, they had actually taken over Lahore, the capital city of Punjab. We cannot talk of Sikh martyrdom without however, mentioning the names of Bhai Taru Singh, Bhai Bota Singh and Bhai Garja Singh, the golden examples of Sikh religious integrity and values.

Bhai Taru Singh

During the reign of Moghul emperor Mohammed Shah, Nawab Zakariya Khan was appointed the Governor of

Hundreds of Sikhs martyrs were beheaded each day at *Nakha*s, the horse market of Lahore.

Lahore and his specific commission was to 'exterminate the entire Sikh nation'. It was truly a hard time for the Sikhs as their head-hunting was the order of the day. Soldiers, scholars, peasants, shopkeepers, ordinary men, women and children, whoever wore long hair and followed the path of Nanak, were indiscriminately condemned to the same fate. The story of Bhai Taru Singh brings out the zest and fortitude with which the Sikhs sacrificed their heads for the sake of their values.

Bhai Taru Singh, who was only a small farmer, continued supplies to Sikh families when the Moghuls had warned everyone against it. He was captured and brought before the Nawab for this criminal offence for which he was to be punished severely. However his sharp features and overwhelming presence moved the Nawab and he offered him the alternative of allowing his hair to the sheared so that his life could be spared. Taru Singh's reply was, "A Sikh and his hair are inseparable. I can give you my head, but not my hair." And so he bravely did.

Bhai Bota Singh and Bhai Garja Singh

In 1739, it was proclaimed that no Sikh existed in the land. What it meant was that all of them had been massacred. At that time, someone hurled a taunt at Bota Singh that if he were still living then he must have been hiding like a coward.

This taunt was really much too much for him to bear. So, he proclaimed that the Khalsa could not be finished. And to prove what he meant, he took position on the grand trunk road near Amritsar and made a proclamation that from point 'x' to point 'y', the road in question was his sovereign territory and none could pass through it without paying him toll tax. The only arm he had with him was a *lathi* (stick). Not just that, his sole companion was one Bhai Garja Singh. But so pervasive was the Sikh fear that people started paying him the tax, of their own accord.

Finally, frustrated thus, Bota Singh informed the Nawab at Lahore of his sovereign status in order to force the issue. This was too much of an affront for the Nawab to accept. In the end, Bota Singh and Garja Singh died fighting.

Later Martyrs

Similarly, the *Baba*s of the Ghadar movement, the saga of Kamagata Maru led by Baba Gurdit Singh to assert the right of Indians to emigrate to greener pastures, and the efforts of the great revolutionaries in India's Independence struggle mark the Sikh spirit of martyrdom of which Bhagat Singh remains the most shining example.

And then, there were valiant acts like those by Udham Singh who avenged the Jallianwala Baug massacre by

Bhagat Singh, prince among the Indian revolutionary martyrs. This photograph was taken in the Ferozepur jail a little before he was hanged.

shooting General Dyer in London in the heart of British power. And others by the Akali movement that retrieved the Sikh Gurudwaras from the influence of the corrupt *Mahant*s, and the fast-unto-death by *Jathedar* Pheruman to protect the luminous tradition of the Sikh *ardas*, the pledge that once taken has to be fulfilled even with life.

Thus, like moths to a flame, the Sikhs confronted their adversaries in their face and stood by their valiant principles, even at the cost of being charred.

Other Sikh Warriors

The Sikh tradition of heroism in battles is matchless. For generations on end, the Sikh warriors lived on horseback with **Nam** on the lips and spears and swords in hand. Death in battle at the Guru's altar was for them life eternal. That is how the tide of Indian history was turned to restore the Hindu Kush mountain as the natural boundary of India in the West.

Udham Singh who avenged the national shame by shooting General Dyer, the perpetrator of Jallianwala Baug tragedy in London in 1940.

In chronological order we come to the *Misl* period after the Sikhs took on the Moghuls frontally under the Banda. The *Misl* period is the period when the regeneration of Indian arms took place. The organization of these *Misl*s was partially tribal. But their strategy was that *Sardar*s of the Sikh *Misl*s would meet twice a year at Amritsar — one, on the occasion of *Baisakhi* and two, on the occasion of the *Dewali* to discuss important war tactics. The *Misl* period is

93

known for guerrilla kind of warfare in which the Sikh really excelled.

Of their guerrilla tactics, Qazi Noor Mohammed in his "*Jang Namah*" writes, "If their armies take to flight, do not take it as an actual flight. It is a war tactic. Beware, of them a second time. The object of their trick is that when the furious enemy runs after them, it is separated from the main army …. then they turn back to face their pursuer and set fire to water." In the same vein, a Swiss officer of the Moghul army wrote, "Five hundred of Najaf Khan's horse dare not encounter 50 Sikh horsemen." *Dhai Phat* (two and a half wounds) is their favourite strategy. According to this strategy, the first step is finding the weaknesses of the enemy and the second step is engaging them to inflict the maximum damage. The last half-strike is to kill and be killed.

The success of these tactics can be gauged from the fact that Nadir Shah, one of the greatest scourges of Asia to have attacked India, was harassed by the Sikhs on his return journey along the foothills of the Shivalik. They were successful in depriving the Shah of large parts of his booty including Indian artisans and women without facing him in open battle. Then Nadir Shah asked Zakaria Khan as to who these people were and where they lived. The Moghul Governor in attendance replied, "They are rebel *Fakirs* whose saddles are their homes." Upon that, the Shah said, "The day is not far off when these rebels will take possession of the country."

A unit of the Sikh-guerilla fighters in hot pursuit of Nadir Shah whom they harassed no end.

Gradually, the Sikhs became so confident that after the collapse of the Moghul administration in Punjab on the death of Mir Mannu in 1753 they began offering protection or *rakha* on the payment of one-fifth of the revenue. The right of the Sikh *Misls* to offer *rakha* was duly recognized by the *Sarbat* Khalsa (Total assembly of the Khalsa which had much the same authority as the Guru himself) in 1756-57. Its natural consequence was that the Sikh Sardars occupied Lahore in 1765. This is how the *Misls* gradually brought Punjab entirely under their rule until Ranjit Singh officially established the Sikh domain all over Punjab with the Satluj as the border with British India. Now started the golden period of the Sikhs — a natural fructification of the lore of Nanak! In fact, the residents of Lahore, the majority being Muslim, invited Ranjit Singh to take over the city.

Ranjit Singh himself was doubtlessly one of the greatest warrior on the scene. He was hardly 16 when he was chosen by the *Misls* to defend Amritsar against the Afghans. The hallmark of his generalship was that he always led from the front. His passion was such that he had once thrown a bagful of gold coins into the river Indus as an offering before throwing his men and horses into its violent flows for the battle of Naushehra.

Another great warrior was Akali Phula Singh, the Jathedar of the Akal Takht. He was a warrior of tradition, who always fought with great religious fervour. Ranjit Singh often used the ferocious *Nihang*s and Akalis of Phula Singh to create deadly results in battles. For instance, it was the charge of the Akalis and *Nihang*s against the impregnable fort of Multan that brought victory to Ranjit Singh.

However, the greatest General-cum-Administrator in Ranjit Singh's army was Hari Singh Nalwa. In almost all the difficult expeditions, it was Nalwa who was chosen to lead. His two outstanding victories were Multan and Kashmir. In 1836, he built the fort of Jamrud to checkmate the Pathans just at the eastern mouth of the Khyber, He was the person sent by Ranjit Singh to invite Lord William Bentick to Rupar. Such was his dread as a warrior that even when he was no more, the Afghans did not find the courage to attack the fort in which his dead body lay.

The Sikhs maintained their reputation for being great soldiers even during the British rule. They served the empire in several sectors, even outside India. During the two World Wars, the Sikhs were the most decorated soldiers. Many Sikhs in the diaspora are the descendents of these soldiers. At its height, about 15-20% of the entire Indian army during the British times consisted of the Sikhs.

It is important to mention the saga of Saragarhi at this point. The Saragarhi battle is among the eight examples of

The peerless Hari Singh Nalwa who was undoubtedly one of the architects of Ranjit Singh's kingdom.

95

A rare portrait of Maharaja Ranjit
Singh of Lahor Darbar at the height of
his glory

collective heroism in the world, nominated by UNESCO. This is the story:

> A posse of 20 Sikh soldiers headed by a *Havildar* was manning the signal post of Saragarhi when thousands of armed Afghans attacked it. It was a surprise attack, hence, the post was without any reinforcements. Though thoroughly outnumbered, the Sikh garrison decided to fight it out and in the process inflicted heavy casualties on the enemy. It was a battle that could not be won. Even so, they fought to the last man and to the last bullet so much so that even when the 20th soldier died the signal man picked up arms to fight the enemy single-handedly. He managed to kill quite a few attackers before he was killed. This is the only instance in the military history of the British Empire in which all the 21 soldiers of the unit were equally decorated with distinguished services medallions. Over time, a suitable memorial was also erected at the post.

The Sikh soldiers have continued to serve the nation after Independence with the same zeal and courage, and nothing fulfills them more than donning the military uniform.

As Farmers and Colonizers

That Punjab has been the granary or food basket of India is greatly due to the fact that the Sikhs are peerless farmers. A common picture of the proud Sikh farmer emerges when he is seen scanning his ripe crops sitting atop a tractor. It is this then that translates itself into a spontaneous dance of joy: No wonder then that Punjab's vigorous *Bhangra* (the male dance) and the graceful *Giddha* (the female dance) have become popular enough to get adapted into main-stream music. The Sikhs always believe living life to the hilt.

The agricultural prosperity that has come to the villages after the 'green revolution' of the sixties and seventies was a result of this attitude. Senior Sikh generals and bureaucrats almost invariably go back to their villages after retirement and put their knowledge to improve farming. That is why one often finds all kind of technological innovations in their fields.

It was the Sikh's love for soiling his land that converted the 'food-deficit' area of Punjab (India) into a 'food-surplus' one. Not only that, Punjab's prosperity comes from the fact that whatever wealth was earned by her land was poured back into her villages to build colleges and technical institutions by the Sikhs.

In fact, the Sikhs agriculturists never missed opportunity that came their way. In the *terai* (sub-mountainous) area of Uttar Pradesh, huge tracts of land were lying fallow and were infested with wild boars. The Sikh farmers purchased these lands at a very low price, killed the boars, ate them up and developed some of the country's biggest and most prosperous mechanized farms there. In fact, some of these lands are the richest in agricultural output today. It is, therefore, not for nothing that a whole district in the Uttranchal (a new State in the hills of former Uttar Pradesh) has been named as Udham Singh Nagar, commemorating the name of the great Punjab martyr of whom we have referred before.

Thus, the Sikhs, by and large have shown deep integrity to Nanak's path that stands for commitment to life by constantly living in the glory of **Nam**, earning the bread with honest hard labour and participating in the life of the community by sharing whatever one can contribute. It is in their faith to make the world a better place to live, giving them a whole new orientation of life. They are not just set apart because of unshorn hair and outward appearance but in their positive mannerisms as well.

Sikhism is the only religion of the world that gives equal importance to spirituality and material wellbeing. In other words, it has the necessary apparatus to combine change with tradition. Hence, adversity does not derail them. Besides, they hate poverty and all that dehumanizes man. Sikhs are ordained never to brook injustice; they have ever to be ready to defend the righteous cause. Nanak's path is, therefore, a celebration of life with both men and women contributing to it as equal partners, staying within the family.

The one spiritual remedy prescribed to overcome all human weaknesses is that of the **Nam** or the word that ensures end of all suffering.

The immortal *Namdhari* martyrs who were blown up after tying them to the mouths of big cannons.

Let us conclude with these words from the 'Joy' hymn of the Guru Amar Das, the Third Nanak:

> *"The world which appears to you gall and sore,*
> *It is nothing but the expression of God Himself.*
> *It is His image; His rainbow vision."*

The Sikh diaspora

The Sikhs can be categorised as one of the most progressive communities of India. This is mainly due to their high mobility that has them settling all across the globe. It is not surprising to find commercials broadcast in Punjabi on some of the city radio stations abroad.

However, the highwater mark of the Sikh character is their "joie-de-vivre" or zest for life. Perhaps it is implicit in the essence of Nanak's teachings and in the sincere practice of the *Nam*. Hence it may not be out of place to mention that Nanak is a rare exception among the spiritual leaders of India, who broke the traditional taboo of going abroad for promoting his socio-spiritual ideas. And the Sikhs, as its followers, entertain no inhibition on this account. Naturally it has greatly benefited the Sikh community as a whole, the results of which are apparant. Isn't it truly remarkable, that today one out of every ten Sikhs is living abroad even though Punjab is a wholly landlocked area?

Bhai Kanhaiyya: A True Server

This is a unique story of humanitarian treatment given to the enemy soldiers. It comes from the very first major battle fought by the Sikhs under Guru Gobind Singh.

The Moghul forces in league with the Rajput soldiers of the hilly states of Punjab attacked the Anandpur Sahib in 1704. The battle saw a very heavy fighting in which, the Sikhs, though out-numbered inflicted heavy casualties on the enemy. It was the second day of battle. In the course of it, a Sikh, named Bhai Kanhaiyya, was serving water to wounded soldiers dying with agony, exhaustion, thirst and wounds. While doing so, he was making no distinction between friends and foes. For some Sikhs, this action was inexcusable. Thus, a complaint was made to the Guru.

When asked to explain, Kanhaiyya told the Guru, "I see no Moghuls or Sikhs among the suffering. In everyone's face I see only you, O my Guru." And so he was blessed for immortality.

'Na koi Hindu; Na Mussalman'

Nanak's Contemporary Relevance Chapter X

Nanak's philosophy is very relevant to a country like India that is driven by religion. When Nanak proclaimed *'Na koi Hindu; Na Mussalman'* he had found the divine solution to India's great communal divide. His revelation of this simple fact was a result of the proximity he felt to God. What he wanted us to know was that God wanted us to look beyond our religious identities and unite as a human force. In truth, there *was* no Hindu or a Mussalman. So, when we expand on this message in the context of today's world, we find that any talk of 'Clash of Civilizations' as based on religion is entirely man-inspired. To quote Nanak "Only he has the right to call himself religious, who lives in the light of God's word as brought to the earth by prophets of all religions."

There is only one civilization and that is human civilization. Hence, all religions are the branches of one super religion — the religion of man, which Nanak propounded relentlessly. This also means that while all terrorism in the name of religion is a travesty of religion, all talk of one religion being superior to another is senseless and must stop.

He also diagnosed that the major cause of suffering in the world was living on the income of so many, and depriving the poor of their rightful share. His short aphorism *'Krit Karna'* and *'Wand Chhakna'*, encourages mankind to earn one's bread the hard, honest way and share it with the needy. For, the hard-earned bread is full of nectar and the exploiter's bread is full of blood.

It is the avarice of some who consider themselves more equal than the rest, that deprive the rightful owners of their due and create an imbalance in the society. Interestingly, Nanak had propounded this very basic thought much before Marx came upon the scene. In fact, this very principle can found a new world order free of exploitation so that the world's resources are shared more equitably.

As Nanak says:

> *"That which belongs to another*
> *Is unlawful like the flesh of a pig to a Mussalman*
> *And the cow's flesh to a Hindu.*
> *The Guru and the Pir will extend their grace*
> *Only if you refrain from eating carrion.*
> *Carrion does not become lawful*
> *By breathing God's name over it.*
> . . . .
> *"The fruit of false talk is falsehood.*
> *Only good deeds open the road to salvation."*

Nanak's magnanimity also lies in the fact that even when he is concerned with the Permanent, he does not shun Change. Sikhism has the capacity to absorb change into tradition and it is through this apparatus that Nanak has introduced a total way of life to people: An ultimate Reality of which permanence and change are integral parts.

A unique aspect of Nanak's philosophy is his denounciation of those who turn their backs on the world of commitment to seek their individual salvation. In his thinking, it is these runaways of life who make this world a place unsuitable to live in. He tends to use an unusual theraphy on the minds of people to bring out the hidden powers of the whole community by the magic of the *Nam*. This clarity in thought helps heals the society and not just the individual. Expression and not inhibition is the cardinal *mantra* of his creed.

The principle question is: Does a collective sub-conscious exist that can really be awakened? Through Sikhism, Nanak created one of the greatest instruments of awakening the total sub-conscious of a whole society. Infact, some of the noblest saintly men, warriors, martyrs, colonizers, farmers, entrepreneurs and sportsmen come from the ranks of his followers.

Going a step further, Nanak becomes relevant to us as one of the greatest Management Gurus. By moulding human life and activity through the path of Sikhism, he brought phenomenal results into society at large, and that too in an age when the concept of management was unheard of.

The world has much to learn from the corporate nature of Sikhism that has grown gradually into a living institution in form of the Sikh Gurudwara. With religion becoming a dwindling force in most contemporary situations, Sikhism promises to shine brighter in its true essence.

Still, the Sikhs are not fundamentalists. They are tolerant and even respectful of all other paths of worship. Besides, everyone is welcome to the Gurdwara without any distinction whatsoever. When a Sikh is within the precincts of the Gurdwara, he is in the presence and protection of none other than Nanak himself. And this confers upon him some unique characteristics. Some of these virtues are humanity, honour and truthfulness to God.

The young *Panj Piara*s leading a Sikh procession, betokening the bright future of Sikhism – the religion of Ten Nanak.

And lastly, Nanak made family the source of all spirituality. In many developed nations of the West, sociologists are much worried at the break down of the family as an institution. The result is an unprecedented wave of anarchy and immorality of sex, crime and violence, sweeping away all the good sense a human being is known for. Nanak asks to revive the family as a value. It is something fundamental to him; it is the fulcrum of all that is positive among human beings. This is where his philosophy is even more relevant than ever before. It is something that concerns the future of human race as a whole.

Nanak's Philosophy of the *Nam*   Epilogue

Nanak's philosophy of the **Nam** is holistic. It is not just the muttering of the sacred word but follows the totality of whatever Nanak stands for. For example, in its subtle form, the **Nam** is beyond time, space and causation; in its gross form, it stands for 'nature', which means the entire world of phenomenon; and between the two, it stands for all the processes of creation.

However, readers may find the Hindu analogy on the subject as quite enlightening to undo the knot. For, in the beginning of time, the Lord God (Formless) is supposed to have breathed in the voids of the space what we know as the *Nada Brahma*. It is this *Nada Brahma*, which then got amplified in the form of the *Veda*, the knowledge illimitable and immaculate. And it is this *Nada Brahma* again, which, it is believed, also got concretized into the cosmos. This is the basis of Hindu cosmology, which today even the official cosmology may not reject out of hand.

What is the *Nada Brahma*? It is commonly understood that its articulate form is *Aum*. It is said that when we start to pronounce the first syllable of this mystic word, it ushers in the beginning of the cosmos because the mouth opens with it. Similarly, its last syllable, with which the mouth gets shut, stands for complete apocalypse or the end of the creation. Thus, it is between these two extremes that all the phenomena of creation are believed to occur. Nanak, the founder of Sikhism, holds the same cosmological concepts. (See the rendition of *Japuji* in the Annexure One).

Nanak's **Nam** is almost parallel to this analogy. For example, *Ek Onkar* of Nanak appears to stand for the *Nada Brahma* and has all the dynamics of the **Nam** built into it. That's what turns the Transcendent into the Immanent or the Formless God into the Personal One. Hence, according to Guru Arjan, Sri Guru Granth Sahib, the Sikh Bible, is nothing but the amplification of *Ek Onkar* only. After all, one of the basic aphorisms of Sikhism is, *"Ek Nam te sab jag banio Khand, Brahmand, Sharir"*.

Translated it would read: From the **Nam** alone came into being the entire creation, which means all the regions of the universe, and the cosmos and even the human body.

Thus if Lord Brahma, the singer of the *Veda*s, is the Guru and all the Hindus are his Sikhs, then the secret word **Aum** is His **Nam** in the Hindu tradition, as it is in the Sikh tradition. Besides, *Aum* has several meanings and contextual usages.

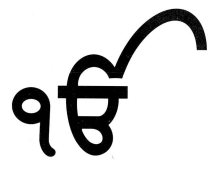

Ek Onkar

Aum

Let us now look at the main areas that constitute the Nanak's philosophy of *Nam*:

(1) Divine Ordination and Revelation

Two things must be understood at the very outset in this context. First, The God Almighty Himself had ordained Nanak to show to the fugitives of the world the true path of God and religion. Secondly, He revealed to Nanak the dynamic instrument of the *Nam* whereby Nanak's disciples or the Sikhs could realize Him with ease.

(2) Nanak's Unique Concepts of God

The *Mool Mantra* or the basic surd of Sikhism, which defines Nanak's God, is as under:

> "Ek Onkar, Satnam(u), Karta Purukh(u), Nirbhau, Nirvair(u), Akal Murat(i), Ajuni, Saibhang, Gur Prasad(I)"

Translated it means: God is one. He is absolute and unique. The *Nam* (not name) alone is His essence. He is the sole Creator. He fears none (Nor does He fill anyone with fear). He hates none (Nor does He fills anyone with hatred). He is timeless or in other words not bound by time and space. He is above and beyond the process of birth and death or even cause and effect. He is self-evident which means He alone knows Himself and He can be realized only through the grace of the Guru. (Here the word Guru does not exclude the Lord Himself).

Let us try to interpret the *Mool Mantra* in terms of his one-point mission: 'There's no Hindu; there's no Mussalman'. As at the face of it, there appears to be nothing new in the above definition of God. But Nanak goes much beyond that any Prophet or Man of God had visualized thus far, thinking beyond religious definition of man.

(3) The Dynamic *Nam*

Nanak says that the absolute formless God is the God before the creation of the cosmos, thus making the entire evolution of cosmos both divine and dynamic through the unique magic wand of the *Nam*. Nanak clearly postulates that the *Nam* is the only manifestation of God in the creation. In fact, for the Sikh Gurus, the *Nam* is like the discipline of the heartbeat. Nothing does or can exist without it. Many call Sikhism as the *Nam Marg* or the way of the *Nam*. For example, to repeat, one of the basic aphorisms of Sikhism is:

> "Ek **Nam** te sab jag banio Khand, Brahmand, Sharir"

(The entire creation has come into existence from the *Nam*; all the regions, the cosmos and the human body.)

Nanak further emphasizes the over-riding importance of the *Nam* as under:

> "O Man! Dwell on the **Nam** — the all-pervading divine spirit and thus return to your eternal home with honour and glory."

(4) Evolution through the *Nam*

Hence, Nanak gives the most dynamic position to the *Nam* in the process of evolution. Without it, even the Absolute God Himself could not have done anything. Hence, the *Nam* is the essence of God's divine and dynamic power that makes the Unmanifest as the Manifest. And if God Himself manifests in creation and the cosmos, then there is nothing left in God's scheme of things that's unreal or unspiritual. And if so, then man as the roof and crown of His creation becomes absolutely central to the spiritual drama that God in His will and grace is directing and enjoying.

Thus, in Sikhism, God and the world both are real. The world is not an empty dream that one has to shun or run away from or a bubble that would burst at the slighest pricking. In fact, every relationship of man in Sikhism is for real. Conversely speaking, the world becomes unreal only if one fails to appreciate and comprehend the power of the *Nam*.

Many scholars of Islam often claim that Nanak has shaped his God after the God of Islam. He is not only the doer but also is all-powerful, overflowing with His solicitousness and grace for the faithful. But by defining God as without fear and hatred, Nanak rejected the Semitic view of God who is both jealous and has to be feared. Besides, Nanak rejects the intercessionary role of the Prophet as standing between man and God. He also rejects limiting God's grace to the faithful only. Hence, his God is the God of the entire creation.

(5) Nanak's Concept of Man

Thus, in Nanak's scheme of things, man stands in a very special relationship with God. For, to re-emphasize through the power of the *Nam*, the Transcendent God becomes Personal and Immanent to man. And thereby He becomes his friend, philosopher and guide. And what God wants man to do is that he should endeavour hard to come back to Him or merge back into the source or into Him in full glory. For, that's the purpose and object of God manifesting Himself in His creation. Or, this is the aim of the life spiritual as it is.

And it can happen. It is said that man, the soul manifested, has already gone through countless births (say, 8.4 million species) that have progressively transmuted themselves into the human form. Thus man has to carefully remove the dust of sense-born desires from the soul so that it shines back in its pristine purity. And this can happen only through the alchemy of the *Nam*.

That is why Nanak cuts all what hell and heaven mean in Semitic religions. He also cuts out any dialectical relationship that God may bear with Mammon. Not just that, he also rejects all paths of *Yogis*, *Sanyasis*, *Bairagis*, *Sufis*, etc. as unspiritual. He roundly admonishes the different sects of ascetics who are known to instil fear and awe in the fugitive man through the demonstration of the supernatural. And he disparages the run-aways of life that leave the world leader-less. If the *Siddha* ascetics found the world too ugly a place to live in, then its onus lay with men like themselves to salvage the world by taking up its leadership.

He rejects the efficacy of ritualistic fasts and pilgrimages. He wants man to refrain from idol-worship as he feels it hampers spiritual evolvement. He makes man responsible for his fall from the heaven as one may call it, by serving the Self through sense-generated desires. In fact, Nanak makes a clear distinction between spirit and Self. He makes *'houme'* or *'egotistic self-seeking'* as the greatest enemy of man. And that *'houme'* is nowhere but within man himself. Hence, man through the agency of the **Nam** has to cure himself of his *'houme'*.

In effect, Nanak's ideal man is *'Sachiara'*, the one ever truthful. He becomes *'Sachiara'* first by becoming *Gurmukh* or Guru-oriented or then a member of the *'Sadh Sangat'* or the holy congregation. And what are his tools? Two tools in the main: One is truthful living and the other is constantly practising the **Nam***-simran*. For example, Nanak in his *Japuji* says:

> *"The Guru has unravelled one great mystery*
> *(Which is) that there's but One benefactor of all creatures.*
> *May I never forget Him —*
> *This is **simran**, this is repetition of the divine **Nam**."*

A Nanak's Sikh has to learn to live in the holy presence of the Lord from dawn to dusk. This is called the **Nam***-simran*. With each breath of his, he has to rhythmically remember the Lord. It is in this sense that **Nam***-simran* becomes the *Jap-yajna* of the Gita. For, it is not for nothing that Lord Krishna says: "Among all the *Yajnas* (sacrifices), I am the *Jap-yajna* — highest of the *Yajnas*!"

It is but proper, therefore, that Guru Nanak exalts the **Nam** to the status of a divine commandment. Says he:

> *"Eko **Nam** Hukam Hai Sat-guru dia bujhai jio."*

> *(To contemplate upon the **Nam** is, verily, the Lord's commandment and this fact has been made evident to me by the true Guru Himself.)*

Nanak also defines the purpose of man's life which is to 'cross the ocean of life' and thus end his spiritual wanderings when now God has given him the opportunity to do so. But he is saddened by the fact that he is wasting this golden opportunity and running after the fulfilment of false desires. His following lines make the message clear:

"Sleeping through man wastes the night;
Eating he wastes the day away;
And thus the jewel of life is bartered away for a trite.
*He who knows not the path of **Nam***
Regrets he, the ignorant man, in the end."

This is the same as most saints and sages have said all through the ages. See how Kabir puts it:

"The human life is rare and precious.
This is not obtained again and again,
As the ripened fruit once fallen
Cannot be attached back to the tree."

(6) Aroused Social Conscience

Nanak's philosophy of the **Nam** is one of aroused social conscience. It does not aim at the emancipation of a single individual but of the entire society. And this emancipation is not just religious and spiritual, it is all-inclusive in that it means to put an end to all forms of tyranny, exploitation and slavery. That's how Sikhism as a revolutionary movement of protest finally came into mortal conflict with the Moghuls.

The greatest contribution of Sikhism in terms of social engineering lies in: (1) undoing the stranglehold of caste system that had divided the society into many closed compartments by making it irrelevant; and (2) giving the women their due place in and out of home. And both of them are indeed revolutionary achievements in the context of the highly stratified Indian society.

The first achievement was the creation of free community kitchen or *Langar* as they call it, as part of the spiritual service. This *Guru-ka-langar* has also been euphemistically named as the temple of food. It demolished blind ritualism, caste restrictions and code of several eating and drinking taboos that had held the bulk of Indian society in thraldom.

This institution is also called *pangat* or sitting in a common holy file. Guru Amar Das, the third Guru, had made it compulsory for anyone coming for an audience with him; he could do so only after he had partaken of the *langar*. And even emperor Akbar, gladly partook of the *langar* before he could actually see the Guru.

Hindus or Muslims, Brahmins or *Shudras*, rich or poor — all had to share their food in *Guru-ka-langar*. And it gained such popularity that it began to be said, 'first *pangat* and then *sangat*'. So, without uttering even a single polemic, Nanak made one of the most rigid social institutions the Hindus knew, yield to the intended social reform. It promoted a new kind of social amity among the Sikhs as well.

Likewise, the status of women in the Hindu society was pitiably low. When the husband died, the widow, either on her own accord, or through coercive pressure of those around, had to jump on his burning pyre. It was indeed very callous and cruel. The Sikh Gurus, particularly Guru Amar Das, carried on a relentless campaign against the *Sati*. Now coupled with the teachings of Nanak, the Sikh women started to get their due place in society. They were now no longer considered inferior to their menfolk.

Similarly, the Sikh Gurus banned infanticide of the girl child that was widely practised in those days. The strict Guru injunction was that no Sikh would have any social relations with the one culpable of female infanticide.

(7) Family as the Source and Fount of all Divinity

As stated above, Nanak launched a powerful attack on those, who in the name of spirituality, would run away from the life of a householder. And this naturally brought the institution of family to the centre-stage of all spirituality. In other words, it meant that women were now to be the source and fount of all pursuits of divinity. For, it was the woman alone that gave meaning and substance to all relationships of the world. Says Nanak:

> *"After the death of one's wife, one seeks another*
> *As through her are the social bonds created.*
> *Why should we condemn the woman,*
> *Who gives birth to the leaders and rulers?*
> *Everyone is born of woman and woman alone;*
> *None, absolutely none, is born otherwise.*
> *God alone is the sole exception to this rule."*

The message could not have been expressed in simpler words. Yet, it was a revolutionary message. Hereafter, the woman was not to be held responsible for man's fall from the kingdom of God. Thus, at one go, Nanak rejected the story of Adam and Eve or even that of the 'original sin'. A man living with his wife faithfullly was in the eyes of Nanak, leading a far more spiritual life than the godly Yogis and *Sanyasis*.

Nanak further exalted the status of women by counselling men to always show *satkar* or chivalry and courtesy to them. But the high point of veneration for women, in his eyes, is the status of *Suhagan*, which means married and enjoying the full measure of her husband's love. This also implies that women too have to learn to be their husbands' beloveds.

This paved the way of what Nanak calls *"Ghar Vich Udas"* or detachment in commitment. Hence, the new metaphor for the pious householder became the 'lotus'; born from muck but still remaining untainted by it. *'Jeevanmukta'* or liberated while still living, became another metaphor for such men.

(8) Nanak's Simple and Practical Life-ethics

Nanak also worked out a simple life-ethics for people of the world to follow. He believed that the elaborate commandments of other organized religions, could be practised mainly in their negation, since they often led to a life of hypocrisy, duplicity and falsehood. Besides, it gave coercive powers to the priestcraft.

Thus, in his own path he put down the following life-ethics: (1) *Nam japana* or chanting the **Nam** as the means of constantly living in God's presence; (2) *Krit karana* or earning once living the hard, honest way; and (3) *Wand chhakna* or sharing what you have with others who are indeed needy. This also includes the concept of *Seva* or 'service above self'.

Similarly, there are three don'ts of Nanak which are : (1) No adultery; (2) no coveting of the other's wealth; and (3) bearing no ill-will or malice towards anyone. In Nanak's terse language, they are: (1) *par tan*; (2) *par dhan*; and (3) *par ninda,* respectively.

Another aphorism of Nanak's ethical charter of life is *"Nam, Dan, Ishnan"* The first two are covered in the three points above. 'Ishnan', in short, though means taking bath, emphasizes the need for personal, social and environmental cleanliness.

However, the bottomline in his ethical path is never to compromise on truth. For, truth to him was the highest attribute of God Himself. But then Nanak by precept and example sufficiently mellowed it down. In fact, he taught that even the harshest truth must be couched in the sweetest language. Nanak, never used a single harsh word in his life even though he condemned all the duplicity and hypocrisy. That explains why even his worst detractors became his disciples in no time.

Thus, the real meaning of the **Nam** appears to be the comprehensive way of life, which governs all Sikhs. It is this that explains how they night and day stand in the immanence of their Guru himself. The holy atmosphere in each Gurdwara or wherever Sri Guru Granth Sahib is ceremoniously placed, is considered suffused with it. This atmosphere is thus full of the **Nam**.

To reiterate, Nanak's **Nam** is a holistic concept. In its subtle form, it transcends all the three eternities, viz., Time, Space and Causation. In its gross form, it stands for the natural phenomena, which means the manifested body of the Formless. And in between fall all the processes of creation and even dissolution. It is, therefore, not for nothing that Nanak exalts **Nam** to the status of a divine commandment. Says he:

*"Eko **Nam** Hukum Hai Satgur dia bujhai jio."*

Translated it means, "To contemplate upon the *Nam* is verily the Lord's sole commandment". In the hands of Nanak, the *Nam* became a perfect tool of social engineering or what we may describe as the Sikh revolution.

The power of the *Nam* has several forms of description in the Sikh terminology: It is the elixir of the *Nam*; it is the alchemy of the *Nam*; it is the ambrosial bath in the lake of the *Nam*; it is oar of the *Nam* that helps one cross the turbid sea of the world; it is the magic wand of the *Nam*; and it is even the miracle of the *Nam*.

In the end, it may be useful to close this introduction with the quintessential Nanak thought that sums up the Sikh *Ardas* or invocation. It consists of only eight words:

*"Nanak **Nam** Chardi Kala: Tere Bhane Sarbatda Bhala."*

(O Nanak! Repeating constantly the *Nam*, always think and act big and positive. In Thy will and grace, O Lord, lies the wellness of the whole creation.)

The *Japuji*:
The Humanity's Master Prayer

No introduction of Nanak is complete until it brings into focus, howsoever briefly, his master prayer the Japuji, pronounced as the *Japji*, 'u' being silent. Can one imagine a seeker suddenly ushered into the Almighty's presence, enjoying every bit His immense creation in all its majesty and splendour? Normally, it will befuddle him no end, as it is difficult to stand up to that Immense Source of Light, which is infinitely stronger than that of the sun. Moses, they say, lost his very ability to behold Him, face to face. And Arjuna too had to be given the divine sight to behold the cosmic God-form of Lord Krishna.

But Nanak on beholding Him, spontaneously went rapturous with wonder and broke into praising Him. What was so special about Nanak? It was his boundless concern for the entire humanity, gone spiritually fugitive in a thousand ways in the sinful age of *Kaliyuga*. It is this impromptu prayer of Nanak that is known as the Japuji. In fact, God was so pleased with it that He made Nanak His special guest at the '*Sach Khand*', His own abode for 72 hours.

Not just that, He also ordained him as His apostle or '*Gur Parmeshar*', to go into the world to spread his own divine message of oneness of humanity and how it could be achieved through the agency of **Nam**. Thus, the Japuji carries the core of God's own blessings to humanity. It is wholly eclectic and universal. In fact, *"Na koi Hindu na Massalman"* is just a small application of the *Japuji* that is also known as Nanak's 'Sermon of Sultanpur'.

It is this master prayer of the *Japuji* that all the followers of Nanak are enjoined to recite in *Amrit Vela* or the ambrosial hour every morning, after becoming pure and clean in both body and mind. This prayer is individual and not sung in chorus with other devotees.

The result: It brings every Sikh of his into Nanak's imminent protection for the day. Thus, it is the key to explaining the innumerable superhuman acts that the Sikhs have performed through the ages. Not just that, it is with this prayer that Guru Granth Sahib, the sacred Sikh scripture opens. Hence, it is the most sacred piece of Sikh religious literature, say as sacred as the *Quran* is to the Muslims or the *Gita* is to the Hindus. Guru Arjan, the fifth Guru, underlined this point in a telling manner when he said that the entire Guru Granth Sahib is just an exposition of the *Japuji* only.

In fact, the *Japuji* forms the core of the **Nam**, the central point of Nanak's message. It is by no means a short prayer. It opens with the *Mool Mantra*, or the basic surd that by far is the best description of a monotheistic God. It is followed by a short *Sloka*. This *Sloka* is an integral part of the *JAPU* or the *Japuji* and as it also occurs in the *Sukhmani*, it appears to have been added by Guru Arjan, the fifth Lord. The *Japuji* has in all 38 stanzas or *pauris*, which in Panjabi means steps or stairs of upward spiritual transcendence which a seeker has to climb in order to achieve liberation. And finally it ends in another short *Sloka* or the concluding verse that ideally sums up the master prayer. This *Sloka* is said to be the work of Guru Angad, the second Sikh Lord.

The subject matter of the *Japuji* is as philosophical as it is analytical. The prayer is terse in style, dense in thought-content and archaic in language. Hence, it is not always easy to follow, much less absorb it. However, its constant repetition each day of one's life overtime makes it a part of one's consciousness. It is, verily, like the *Yoga* that practised over long years ultimately fills the mind with divine knowledge, helping one to reach his destination, leading to liberation, realization and enlightenment.

Here is a simple and literal rendition of the *Japuji* into Engligh for three reasons: One, it is a prayer essentially supplicatory, marked with humility and wonder before the matchless grandeur of god; two, it is spontaneous and appears truly sparked off by the limitless majesty of God Himself. In fact, it looks it descended on Nanak like a torrent; and three, it reflects the breadth of Nanak's total vision and thought at one go. In fact, if we study it closely, it also encompasses the whole spiritual agenda of Sikhism. Towards the end, it also alludes to how the simple *Bhakta*s get transformed into saint soldiers. It happens when they enter the last stage of spiritual transcendence of man and experience true proximity to God.

Ek Onkar, Satnam(u), Karta Purukh(u),
Nirbhau, Nirvair(u), Akal Murat(i),
Ajuni, Saibhang, Gur Prasad(I)

(For its translation: please see under para (2) of
the Epilogue which is Philosophy of the *Nam*.)

ੴ ਸਤਿ ਨਾਮੁ ਕਰਤਾ ਪੁਰਖ
ਨਿਰਭਉ ਨਿਰਵੈਰੁ ਅਕਾਲ ਮੂਰਤਿ
ਅਜੂਨੀ ਸੈਭੰ ਗੁਰ ਪ੍ਰਸਾਦਿ ॥

एक ओंकार सति नामु
करता पुरखु निरभउ निरवैरु
अकाल मूरति अजूनी सैभं
गुर प्रसादि॥

JAPU

In the beginning of time, He was the Truth. In all
the ages since then, He remained the Truth.
O Nanak! In the present time He alone in the
Truth.
And in times to come, He will be nothing but the
Truth, eternal and ever.

ਆਦਿ ਸਚੁ ਜੁਗਾਦਿ ਸਚੁ ॥
ਹੈ ਭੀ ਸਚੁ ਨਾਨਕ ਹੋਸੀ ਭੀ ਸਚੁ ॥੧॥

आदि सचु जुगादि सचु ॥
है भी सचु नानक होसी भी सचु ॥

Pauri One

Not by bathing a hundred thousand times is one
rendered pure.
(Alternatively: Not by thought alone, however
intense, can He be realized)
Not by observing silence endlessly can one
achieve inner silence (Samadhi).
Not by eating howsoever dainty be the dishes can
one mitigate the hunger of
the soul.
Howsoever thoughtful a man might be, no
thought can take one to his spiritual
destination.
How then to become a 'Sachiara' to pierce
falsehood and know Him, the Eternal Truth?
O Nanak! God can be known only by abiding by
His will.

ਸੋਚੈ ਸੋਚਿ ਨ ਹੋਵਈ
ਜੇ ਸੋਚੀ ਲਖ ਵਾਰ ॥
ਚੁਪੈ ਚੁਪ ਨ ਹੋਵਈ
ਜੇ ਲਾਇ ਰਹਾ ਲਿਵਤਾਰ ॥
ਭੁਖਿਆ ਭੁਖ ਨ ਉਤਰੀ
ਜੇ ਬੰਨਾ ਪੁਰੀਆ ਭਾਰ ॥
ਸਹਸ ਸਿਆਣਪਾ ਲਖ ਹੋਹਿ
ਤ ਇਕ ਨ ਚਲੈ ਨਾਲਿ ॥
ਕਿਵ ਸਚਿਆਰਾ ਹੋਈਐ
ਕਿਵ ਕੂੜੈ ਤੁਟੈ ਪਾਲਿ ॥
ਹੁਕਮਿ ਰਜਾਈ ਚਲਣਾ
ਨਾਨਕ ਲਿਖਿਆ ਨਾਲਿ ॥੧॥

सोचै सोचि न होवई
जे सोची लख वार ॥
चुपै चुप न होवई
जे लाइ रहा लिव तार ॥
भुखिआ भुख न उतरी
जे बंना पुरीआ भार ॥
सहस सिआणपा लख होहि
त इक न चलै नालि ॥
किव सचिआरा होईऐ
किव कूड़ै तुटै पालि ॥
हुकमि रजाई चलणा
नानक लिखिआ नालि ॥१॥

Pauri Two

By His decree alone are all beings created. But
none knows how it operates.
By Him ordered do we come into the world and
are blessed with greatness.
By His ordinance do we become high or low or
enjoy pleasure or pain.
By His grace do some reach excellence and others
disgraced.
His decree alone covers all; none is outside it.
O Nanak! If alone someone knows it all to be the
working of His will,
Then none whatsoever shall suffer from ego or
I-amness.

ਹੁਕਮੀ ਹੋਵਨਿ ਆਕਾਰ
ਹੁਕਮੁ ਨ ਕਹਿਆ ਜਾਈ ॥
ਹੁਕਮੀ ਹੋਵਨਿ ਜੀਅ
ਹੁਕਮਿ ਮਿਲੈ ਵਡਿਆਈ ॥
ਹੁਕਮੀ ਉਤਮੁ ਨੀਚੁ
ਹੁਕਮਿ ਲਿਖਿ ਦੁਖ ਸੁਖ ਪਾਈਅਹਿ ॥
ਇਕਨਾ ਹੁਕਮੀ ਬਖਸੀਸ
ਇਕਿ ਹੁਕਮੀ ਸਦਾ ਭਵਾਈਅਹਿ ॥
ਹੁਕਮੈ ਅੰਦਰਿ ਸਭੁ ਕੋ
ਬਾਹਰਿ ਹੁਕਮ ਨ ਕੋਇ ॥
ਨਾਨਕ ਹੁਕਮੈ ਜੇ ਬੁਝੈ
ਤ ਹਉਮੈ ਕਹੈ ਨ ਕੋਇ ॥੨॥

हुकमी होवनि आकार
हुकमु न कहिआ जाई ॥
हुकमी होवनि जीअ
हुकमि मिलै वडिआई ॥
हुकमी उतमु नीचु
हुकमि लिखि दुख सुख पाईअहि ॥
इकना हुकमी बखसीस
इकि हुकमी सदा भवाईअहि ॥
हुकमै अंदरि सभु को
बाहरि हुकम न कोइ ॥
नानक हुकमै जे बुझै
त हउमै कहै न कोई ॥२॥

113

How can we sing praises to
  His effulgence?
How can we measure the plenitude of
  His greatness?
How can we estimate the value of four
  excellences that He confers?
How can we know the source of one's knowledge
  and good and bad thoughts?
How can we praise Him as being the Creator and
  the Destroyer?
How do we know that remembering
  Him one does not become pauper?
In fact, there are no words that can truly describe
  His bounties.
How to know then that He never tires of giving
  though we may tire of receiving?
Through the endless ages on His bounty alone
  has the creation survived.
From time immemorial, He has maintained His
  order through
  His grace only.
And that's how He is eternally full of joy and
  ever so cheerful.

ਗਾਵੈ ਕੋ ਤਾਣੁ ਹੋਵੈ ਕਿਸੈ ਤਾਣੁ ॥
ਗਾਵੈ ਕੋ ਦਾਤਿ ਜਾਣੈ ਨੀਸਾਣੁ ॥
ਗਾਵੈ ਕੋ ਗੁਣ ਵਡਿਆਈਆ ਚਾਰ ॥
ਗਾਵੈ ਕੋ ਵਿਦਿਆ ਵਿਖਮੁ ਵੀਚਾਰੁ ॥
ਗਾਵੈ ਕੋ ਸਾਜਿ ਕਰੇ ਤਨੁ ਖੇਹ ॥
ਗਾਵੈ ਕੋ ਜੀਅ ਲੈ ਫਿਰਿ ਦੇਹ ॥
ਗਾਵੈ ਕੋ ਜਾਪੈ ਦਿਸੈ ਦੂਰਿ ॥
ਗਾਵੈ ਕੋ ਵੇਖੈ ਹਾਦਰਾ ਹਦੂਰਿ ॥
ਕਥਨਾ ਕਥੀ ਨ ਆਵੈ ਤੋਟਿ ॥
ਕਥਿ ਕਥਿ ਕਥੀ ਕੋਟੀ ਕੋਟਿ ਕੋਟਿ ॥
ਦੇਦਾ ਦੇ ਲੈਦੇ ਥਕਿ ਪਾਹਿ ॥
ਜੁਗਾ ਜੁਗੰਤਰਿ ਖਾਹੀ ਖਾਹਿ ॥
ਹੁਕਮੀ ਹੁਕਮੁ ਚਲਾਏ ਰਾਹੁ ॥
ਨਾਨਕ ਵਿਗਸੈ ਵੇਪਰਵਾਹੁ ॥੩॥

गावै को ताणु होवै किसै ताणु ॥
गावै को दाति जाणै नीसाणु ॥
गावै को गुण वडिआईआ चार ॥
गावै को विदिआ विखमु वीचारु ॥
गावै को साजि करे तनु खेह ॥
गावै को जीअ लै फिरि देह ॥
गावै को जापै दिसै दूरि ॥
गावै को वेखै हादरा हदूरि ॥
कथना कथी न आवै तोटि ॥
कथि कथि कथी कोटी कोटि कोटि॥
देदा दे लैदे थकि पाहि ॥
जुगा जुगंतरि खाही खाहि ॥
हुकमी हुकमु चलाए राहु ॥
नानक विगसै वेपरवाहु ॥३॥

True is the Lord and true His *Nam* that is to be
  repeated all the time.
All the creatures cry all the time, "O Lord! Give
  us, give us".
But He, the Bountiful never, never says no.
Then how to repeat His *Nam* so that we see His
  court above?
How to learn the speech that may fill
  Him with love and compassion?
In the ambrosial hour we must ponder over His
  true *Nam* and greatness.
Remember! The path of action ends only in
  perpetuating the cycle of births and deaths.
Liberation comes only when He showers
  His grace.
Hence O Nanak! He alone knows His true ways.

ਸਾਚਾ ਸਾਹਿਬੁ ਸਾਚੁ ਨਾਇ
ਭਾਖਿਆ ਭਾਉ ਅਪਾਰੁ ॥
ਆਖਹਿ ਮੰਗਹਿ ਦੇਹਿ ਦੇਹਿ
ਦਾਤਿ ਕਰੇ ਦਾਤਾਰੁ ॥
ਫੇਰਿ ਕਿ ਅਗੈ ਰਖੀਐ
ਜਿਤੁ ਦਿਸੈ ਦਰਬਾਰੁ ॥
ਮੁਹੌ ਕਿ ਬੋਲਣੁ ਬੋਲੀਐ
ਜਿਤੁ ਸੁਣਿ ਧਰੇ ਪਿਆਰੁ ॥
ਅੰਮ੍ਰਿਤ ਵੇਲਾ ਸਚੁ ਨਾਉ
ਵਡਿਆਈ ਵੀਚਾਰੁ ॥
ਕਰਮੀ ਆਵੈ ਕਪੜਾ
ਨਦਰੀ ਮੋਖੁ ਦੁਆਰੁ ॥
ਨਾਨਕ ਏਵੈ ਜਾਣੀਐ
ਸਭੁ ਆਪੇ ਸਚਿਆਰੁ ॥੪॥

साचा साहिबु साचु नाइ
भाखिआ भाउ अपारु ॥
आखहि मंगहि देहि देहि
दाति करे दातारु ॥
फेरि कि अगे रखीऐ
जितु दिसै दरबारु ॥
मुहौ कि बोलणु बोलीऐ
जितु सुणि धरे पिआरु ॥
अंमृित वेला सचु नाउ
वडिआई वीचारु ॥
करमी आवै कपड़ा
नदरी मोखु दुआरु ॥
नानक एवै जाणीऐ
सभु आपे सचिआरु ॥४॥

He cannot be installed; He cannot be created by
any effort.

He is above all matter; He is self-existent

Whoever has served Him is fully rewarded.

Nanak! Praise Him we must as He permeates all
dimensions.

Also remember! He is the invisible excellence in
every heart.

Let He be praised as He presides over your inner
self.

Endless is the sorrow that makes short work of
pleasure.

God is the eternal sound (*Nam*) as God is the
knowledge incarnate.

It's in the *Nam* then that God expresses Himself.

Whether Ishwar or Brahma or Gorakh or the
Goddess Parbati—

All the Gurus always praised Him alone.

Those who know cannot tell and those that tell
do not know.

The point is that that God is the great riddle.

However, don't ever forget that God alone is the
sole provider.

So, forget Him not even for a moment.

ਥਾਪਿਆ ਨ ਜਾਇ ਕੀਤਾ ਨ ਹੋਇ ॥
ਆਪੇ ਆਪਿ ਨਿਰੰਜਨੁ ਸੋਇ ॥
ਜਿਨਿ ਸੇਵਿਆ ਤਿਨਿ ਪਾਇਆ ਮਾਨੁ ॥
ਨਾਨਕ ਗਾਵੀਐ ਗੁਣੀ ਨਿਧਾਨੁ ॥
ਗਾਵੀਐ ਸੁਣੀਐ ਮਨਿ ਰਖੀਐ ਭਾਉ ॥
ਦੁਖੁ ਪਰਹਰਿ ਸੁਖੁ ਘਰਿ ਲੈ ਜਾਇ ॥
ਗੁਰਮੁਖਿ ਨਾਦੰ ਗੁਰਮੁਖਿ ਵੇਦੰ
ਗੁਰਮੁਖਿ ਰਹਿਆ ਸਮਾਈ ॥
ਗੁਰੁ ਈਸਰੁ ਗੁਰੁ ਗੋਰਖੁ ਬਰਮਾ
ਗੁਰੁ ਪਾਰਬਤੀ ਮਾਈ ॥
ਜੇ ਹਉ ਜਾਣਾ ਆਖਾ ਨਾਹੀ
ਕਹਣਾ ਕਥਨੁ ਨ ਜਾਈ ॥
ਗੁਰਾ ਇਕ ਦੇਹਿ ਬੁਝਾਈ ॥
ਸਭਨਾ ਜੀਆ ਕਾ ਇਕੁ ਦਾਤਾ
ਸੋ ਮੈ ਵਿਸਰਿ ਨ ਜਾਈ ॥੫॥

थापिआ न जाइ कीता न होइ ॥
आपे आपि निरंजनु सोइ ॥
जिनि सेविआ तिनि पाइआ मानु ॥
नानक गावीऐ गुणी निधानु ॥
गावीऐ सुणीऐ मनि रखीऐ भाउ ॥
दुखु परहरि सुखु घरि लै जाइ ॥
गुरमुखि नादं गुरमुखि वेदं
गुरमुखि रहिआ समाई ॥
गुरु ईसरु गुरु गोरखु बरमा
गुरु पारबती माई ॥
जे हउ जाणा आखा नाही
कहणा कथनु न जाई ॥
गुरा इक देहि बुझाई ॥
सभना जीआ का इकु दाता
सो मै विसरि न जाई ॥५॥

If ever He is pleased I shall bathe at any
pilgrimage spot.

If He wills it otherwise I shall abjure
from it.

Wisdom lies in knowing that nothing is achieved
without action.

When the true Guru teaches, all rubies,
jewels and gems

Are found buried in your own heart.

Thus the true Guru alone solves the
great riddle.

However, don't ever forget that God alone is the
sole provider

So forget Him not even for a moment.

ਤੀਰਥਿ ਨਾਵਾ ਜੇ ਤਿਸੁ ਭਾਵਾ
ਵਿਣੁ ਭਾਣੇ ਕਿ ਨਾਇ ਕਰੀ ॥
ਜੇਤੀ ਸਿਰਠਿ ਉਪਾਈ ਵੇਖਾ
ਵਿਣੁ ਕਰਮਾ ਕਿ ਮਿਲੈ ਲਈ ॥
ਮਤਿ ਵਿਚਿ ਰਤਨ ਜਵਾਹਰ ਮਾਣਿਕ
ਜੇ ਇਕ ਗੁਰ ਕੀ ਸਿਖ ਸੁਣੀ ॥
ਗੁਰਾ ਇਕ ਦੇਹਿ ਬੁਝਾਈ ॥
ਸਭਨਾ ਜੀਆ ਕਾ ਇਕੁ ਦਾਤਾ
ਸੋ ਮੈ ਵਿਸਰਿ ਨ ਜਾਈ ॥੬॥

तीरथि नावा जे तिसु भावा
विणु भाणे कि नाइ करी ॥
जेती सिरठि उपाई वेखा
विणु करमा कि मिलै लई ॥
मति विचि रतन जवाहर माणिक
जे इक गुर की सिख सुणी ॥
गुरा इक देहि बुझाई ॥
सभना जीआ का इकु दाता
सो मै विसरि न जाई ॥६॥

115

Through all the four ages or through many more
  lengths of time
Or through all the nine regions,
Supposing one has walked with great name and
  fame,
But if the same is devoid of His grace,
Not one is there to acknowledge him for
  anything.
Remember! The smallest insect He create, He
  fully provides for.
Hence, what should be known is that a man is
  wise
Only if he is the recipient of His grace.
For, He alone bestows all His bounties.

ਜੋ ਜੁਗ ਚਾਰੇ ਆਰਜਾ
ਹੋਰ ਦਸੂਣੀ ਹੋਇ ॥
ਨਵਾ ਖੰਡਾ ਵਿਚਿ ਜਾਣੀਐ
ਨਾਲਿ ਚਲੈ ਸਭੁ ਕੋਇ ॥
ਚੰਗਾ ਨਾਉ ਰਖਾਇ ਕੈ
ਜਸੁ ਕੀਰਤਿ ਜਗਿ ਲੇਇ ॥
ਜੇ ਤਿਸੁ ਨਦਰਿ ਨ ਆਵਈ
ਤ ਵਾਤ ਨ ਪੁਛੈ ਕੇ ॥
ਕੀਟਾ ਅੰਦਰਿ ਕੀਟੁ ਕਰਿ
ਦੋਸੀ ਦੋਸੁ ਧਰੇ ॥
ਨਾਨਕ ਨਿਰਗੁਣਿ ਗੁਣੁ ਕਰੇ
ਗੁਣਵੰਤਿਆ ਗੁਣੁ ਦੇ ॥
ਤੇਹਾ ਕੋਇ ਨ ਸੁਝਈ
ਜਿ ਤਿਸੁ ਗੁਣੁ ਕੋਇ ਕਰੇ ॥੭॥

जे जुग चारे आरजा
होर दसूणी होइ ॥
नवा खंडा विचि जाणीऐ
नालि चलै सभु कोइ ॥
चंगा नाउ रखाइ कै
जसु कीरति जगि लेइ ॥
जे तिसु नदरि न आवई
त वात न पुछै के ॥
कीटा अंदरि कीटु करि
दोसी दोसु धरे ॥
नानक निरगुणि गुणु करे
गुणवंतिआ गुणु दे ॥
तेहा कोइ न सुझई
जि तिसु गुणु कोइ करे ॥७॥

On listening to the *Nam* one achieves the powers
  of an evolved soul;
On listening to the *Nam* all mysteries of the
  Cosmos are revealed;
On listening to the *Nam* nothing is left unknown
  in the upper and lower regions;
On listening to the *Nam* one conquers the fear of
  death:
On listening to the *Nam* a *Bhakta* is lost ever in
  ecstasy;
On listening to the *Nam* disappear all the sins
  and sorrows of the world.

ਸੁਣਿਐ ਸਿਧ ਪੀਰ ਸੁਰਿ ਨਾਥ ॥
ਸੁਣਿਐ ਧਰਤਿ ਧਵਲ ਆਕਾਸ ॥
ਸੁਣਿਐ ਦੀਪ ਲੋਅ ਪਾਤਾਲ ॥
ਸੁਣਿਐ ਪੋਹਿ ਨ ਸਕੈ ਕਾਲੁ ॥
ਨਾਨਕ ਭਗਤਾ ਸਦਾ ਵਿਗਾਸੁ ॥
ਸੁਣਿਐ ਦੂਖ ਪਾਪ ਕਾ ਨਾਸੁ ॥੮॥

सुणिऐ सिध पीर सुरि नाथ ॥
सुणिऐ धरति धवल आकास ॥
सुणिऐ दीप लोअ पाताल ॥
सुणिऐ पोहि न सकै कालु ॥
नानक भगता सदा विगासु ॥
सुणिऐ दूख पाप का नासु ॥८॥

Says Nanak: On listening to the *Nam* one gets
  exalted to the status of gods;
On listening to the *Nam* even the
  dim-witted are praised for their wisdom;
On listening to the *Nam* become evident the
  secrets of Yoga, body and mind;
On listening to the *Nam* is known the sacred
  knowledge of the world;
On listening to the *Nam* a *Bhakta* is lost ever in
  ecstasy;
On listening to the *Nam* disappear all the sins
  and sorrows of the world.

ਸੁਣਿਐ ਈਸਰੁ ਬਰਮਾ ਇੰਦੁ ॥
ਸੁਣਿਐ ਮੁਖਿ ਸਾਲਾਹਣ ਮੰਦੁ ॥
ਸੁਣਿਐ ਜੋਗ ਜੁਗਤਿ ਤਨਿ ਭੇਦ ॥
ਸੁਣਿਐ ਸਾਸਤ ਸਿੰਮ੍ਰਿਤਿ ਵੇਦ ॥
ਨਾਨਕ ਭਗਤਾ ਸਦਾ ਵਿਗਾਸੁ ॥
ਸੁਣਿਐ ਦੂਖ ਪਾਪ ਕਾ ਨਾਸੁ ॥੯॥

सुणिऐ ईसरु बरमा इंदु ॥
सुणिऐ मुखि सालाहण मंदु ॥
सुणिऐ जोग जुगति तनि भेद ॥
सुणिऐ सासत सिम्रिति वेद ॥
नानक भगता सदा विगासु ॥
सुणिऐ दूख पाप का नासु ॥९॥

Pauri Ten

Says Nanak: On listening to the *Nam* are known reality, contentment and wisdom;
On listening to the *Nam*, all pilgrimages stand automatically performed;
On listening to the *Nam*, the learned find distinctions conferred on them;
On listening to the *Nam*, one easily attains the *Sahaj Samadhi*;
On listening to the *Nam*, a *Bhakta* is lost ever in ecstasy;
On listening to the *Nam* disappear all the sins and sorrows of the world.

ਸੁਨਿਐ ਸਤੁ ਸੰਤੋਖੁ ਗਿਆਨੁ ॥
ਸੁਨਿਐ ਅਠਸਠਿ ਕਾ ਇਸਨਾਨੁ ॥
ਸੁਨਿਐ ਪੜਿ ਪੜਿ ਪਾਵਹਿ ਮਾਨੁ ॥
ਸੁਨਿਐ ਲਾਗੈ ਸਹਜਿ ਧਿਆਨੁ ॥
ਨਾਨਕ ਭਗਤਾ ਸਦਾ ਵਿਗਾਸੁ ॥
ਸੁਨਿਐ ਦੂਖ ਪਾਪ ਕਾ ਨਾਸੁ ॥੧੦॥

सुनिऐ सतु संतोखु गिआनु ॥
सुनिऐ अठसठि का इसनानु ॥
सुनिऐ पड़ि पड़ि पावहि मानु ॥
सुनिऐ लागै सहजि धिआनु ॥
नानक भगता सदा विगासु ॥
सुनिऐ दूख पाप का नासु ॥१०॥

Pauri Eleven

Says Nanak: On listening to the *Nam* are earned both truth and wisdom;
On listening to the *Nam* nothing is left unachieved in the mundane and spiritual world;
On listening to the *Nam*, the blind find the right paths;
On listening to the *Nam*, aspirants attain the higher knowledge;
On listening to the *Nam*, a *Bhakta* is lost ever in ecstasy;
On listening to the *Nam* disappear all the sins and sorrows of the world.

ਸੁਨਿਐ ਸਰਾ ਗੁਣਾ ਕੇ ਗਾਹ ॥
ਸੁਨਿਐ ਸੇਖ ਪੀਰ ਪਾਤਿਸਾਹ ॥
ਸੁਨਿਐ ਅੰਧੇ ਪਾਵਹਿ ਰਾਹੁ ॥
ਸੁਨਿਐ ਹਾਥ ਹੋਵੈ ਅਸਗਾਹੁ ॥
ਨਾਨਕ ਭਗਤਾ ਸਦਾ ਵਿਗਾਸੁ ॥
ਸੁਨਿਐ ਦੂਖ ਪਾਪ ਕਾ ਨਾਸੁ ॥੧੧॥

सुनिऐ सरा गुणा के गाह ॥
सुनिऐ सेख पीर पातिसाह ॥
सुनिऐ अंधे पावहि राहु ॥
सुनिऐ हाथ होवै असगाहु ॥
नानक भगता सदा विगासु ॥
सुनिऐ दूख पाप का नासु ॥११॥

Pauri Twelve

There's no end to the achievements of one who ruminates over the *Nam*;
He who runs it down regrets in the end;
No paper and pen can capture what He knows;
Who can comprehend the state of such a one?
For, such a one is truly the immaculate
As he who knows Him needs nothing more to know.

ਮੰਨੇ ਕੀ ਗਤਿ ਕਹੀ ਨ ਜਾਇ ॥
ਜੇ ਕੋ ਕਹੈ ਪਿਛੈ ਪਛੁਤਾਇ ॥
ਕਾਗਦਿ ਕਲਮ ਨ ਲਿਖਣਹਾਰੁ ॥
ਮੰਨੇ ਕਾ ਬਹਿ ਕਰਨਿ ਵੀਚਾਰੁ ॥
ਐਸਾ ਨਾਮੁ ਨਿਰੰਜਨੁ ਹੋਇ ॥
ਜੇ ਕੋ ਮੰਨਿ ਜਾਣੈ ਮਨਿ ਕੋਇ ॥੧੨॥

मंने की गति कही न जाइ ॥
जे को कहै पिछै पछुताइ ॥
कागदि कलम न लिखणहारु ॥
मंने का बहि करनि वीचारु ॥
ऐसा नामु निरंजनु होइ ॥
जे को मंनि जाणै मनि कोइ ॥१२॥

Pauri Thirteen

One who ruminates over the *Nam* transcends both mind and intellect;
One who ruminates over the *Nam* has knowledge of all the worlds;
One who ruminates over the *Nam* does not stumble on the way;
One who ruminates over the *Nam* does not fear the Lord of death;
For such a one is truly the immaculate
As he who knows Him needs nothing more to know.

ਮੰਨੈ ਸੁਰਤਿ ਹੋਵੈ ਮਨਿ ਬੁਧਿ ॥
ਮੰਨੈ ਸਗਲ ਭਵਣ ਕੀ ਸੁਧਿ ॥
ਮੰਨੈ ਮੁਹਿ ਚੋਟਾ ਨਾ ਖਾਇ ॥
ਮੰਨੈ ਜਮ ਕੈ ਸਾਥਿ ਨ ਜਾਇ ॥
ਐਸਾ ਨਾਮੁ ਨਿਰੰਜਨੁ ਹੋਇ ॥
ਜੇ ਕੋ ਮੰਨਿ ਜਾਣੈ ਮਨਿ ਕੋਇ ॥੧੩॥

मंनै सुरति होवै मनि बुधि॥
मंनै सगल भवण की सुधि॥
मंने मुहि चोटा ना खाइ॥
मंनै जम कै साथि न जाइ॥
ऐसा नामु निरंजनु होइ॥
जे को मंनि जाणै मनि कोइ॥१३॥

One who ruminates over the *Nam* does not tire
   on the way;
One who ruminates over the *Nam* has his honour
   unsullied;
One who ruminates over the *Nam* does not
   waver on his path;
One who ruminates over the *Nam* is protected by
   Dharma, the divine law;
For, such a one is truly the immaculate
As he who knows Him needs nothing more
   to know.

ਮੰਨੈ ਮਾਰਗਿ ਠਾਕ ਨ ਪਾਇ ॥
ਮੰਨੈ ਪਤਿ ਸਿਉ ਪਰਗਟੁ ਜਾਇ ॥
ਮੰਨੈ ਮਗੁ ਨ ਚਲੈ ਪੰਥੁ ॥
ਮੰਨੈ ਧਰਮ ਸੇਤੀ ਸਨਬੰਧੁ ॥
ਐਸਾ ਨਾਮੁ ਨਿਰੰਜਨੁ ਹੋਇ ॥
ਜੇ ਕੋ ਮੰਨਿ ਜਾਣੈ ਮਨਿ ਕੋਇ ॥੧੪॥

मंनै मारगि ठाक न पाइ ॥
मंनै पति सिउ परगटु जाइ ॥
मंनै मगु न चलै पंथु ॥
मंनै धरम सेती सनबंधु ॥
ऐसा नामु निरंजनु होइ ॥
जे को मंनि जाणै मनि कोइ ॥१४॥

One who ruminates over the *Nam* attains
   liberation;
One who ruminates over the *Nam* also leads his
   people to liberation;
One who ruminates over the *Nam* saves the
   whole community of disciples;
One who ruminates over the *Nam* needs no
   favours from anyone;
For, such a one is truly the immaculate
As he who knows Him needs nothing more to
   know.

ਮੰਨੈ ਪਾਵਹਿ ਮੋਖੁ ਦੁਆਰੁ ॥
ਮੰਨੈ ਪਰਵਾਰੈ ਸਾਧਾਰੁ ॥
ਮੰਨੈ ਤਰੈ ਤਾਰੇ ਗੁਰੁ ਸਿਖ ॥
ਮੰਨੈ ਨਾਨਕ ਭਵਹਿ ਨ ਭਿਖ ॥
ਐਸਾ ਨਾਮੁ ਨਿਰੰਜਨੁ ਹੋਇ ॥
ਜੇ ਕੋ ਮੰਨਿ ਜਾਣੈ ਮਨਿ ਕੋਇ ॥੧੫॥

मंनै पावहि मोखु दुआरु ॥
मंनै परवारै साधारु ॥
मंनै तरै तारे गुरु सिख ॥
मंनै नानक भवहि न भिख ॥
ऐसा नामु निरंजनु होइ ॥
जे को मंनि जाणै मनि कोइ ॥१५॥

Believers of the *Nam* are the chosen ones
Who win laurels in God's abode.
Such believers shed lustre on the courts of kings.
Constant meditation is the Guru's ordination to
   them.
Whatever they say is the reason itself.
Whatever has the Creator done is beyond
   comprehension.
The fabled bull of *Dharma* that sustains the
   cosmos,
Is, verily, the son of Lord's compassion.
The yoke that binds it is woven with fine strands
   of contentment.
The one who knows it is knower of the truth.
He knows what load this bull of *Dharma* bears.
It not only bears the load of our cosmos,
There are also many more such cosmoses, beyond
   and yonder,
And dutifully it bears the entire load.
But what's the power behind it that makes it
   carry the load?
It's obviously Yours, O Lord!
There are creatures of immense diversity, of
   many a size and colour.
Yet they reflect the same divinity.
Which was the pen that wrote this entire story?
   Who can tell?
How to describe that beauty and might
That with just the help of one *Nam*
Created this whole universe,
With a thousand rivers therein flowing?
How can I praise Thee, O Benevolent.
For, little is my power to do it?
So, whatever is Thy will, I bow before it.
O the Formless one! Thou alone reign,
   for ever and ever.

ਪੰਚ ਪਰਵਾਣ ਪੰਚ ਪਰਧਾਨ ॥
ਪੰਚੇ ਪਾਵਹਿ ਦਰਗਹਿ ਮਾਨੁ ॥
ਪੰਚੇ ਸੋਹਹਿ ਦਰਿ ਰਾਜਾਨੁ ॥
ਪੰਚਾ ਕਾ ਗੁਰੁ ਏਕੁ ਧਿਆਨੁ ॥
ਜੇ ਕੋ ਕਹੈ ਕਰੈ ਵੀਚਾਰੁ ॥
ਕਰਤੇ ਕੈ ਕਰਣੈ ਨਾਹੀ ਸੁਮਾਰੁ ॥
ਧੌਲੁ ਧਰਮੁ ਦਇਆ ਕਾ ਪੂਤੁ ॥
ਸੰਤੋਖੁ ਥਾਪਿ ਰਖਿਆ ਜਿਨਿ ਸੂਤਿ ॥
ਜੇ ਕੋ ਬੁਝੈ ਹੋਵੈ ਸਚਿਆਰੁ ॥
ਧਵਲੈ ਉਪਰਿ ਕੇਤਾ ਭਾਰੁ ॥
ਧਰਤੀ ਹੋਰੁ ਪਰੈ ਹੋਰੁ ਹੋਰੁ ॥
ਤਿਸ ਤੇ ਭਾਰੁ ਤਲੈ ਕਵਣੁ ਜੋਰੁ ॥
ਜੀਅ ਜਾਤਿ ਰੰਗਾ ਕੇ ਨਾਵ ॥
ਸਭਨਾ ਲਿਖਿਆ ਵੁੜੀ ਕਲਾਮ ॥
ਏਹੁ ਲੇਖਾ ਲਿਖਿ ਜਾਣੈ ਕੋਇ ॥
ਲੇਖਾ ਲਿਖਿਆ ਕੇਤਾ ਹੋਇ ॥
ਕੇਤਾ ਤਾਣੁ ਸੁਆਲਿਹੁ ਰੂਪੁ ॥
ਕੇਤੀ ਦਾਤਿ ਜਾਣੈ ਕੌਣੁ ਕੂਤੁ ॥
ਕੀਤਾ ਪਸਾਉ ਏਕੋ ਕਵਾਉ ॥
ਤਿਸ ਤੇ ਹੋਏ ਲਖ ਦਰੀਆਉ ॥
ਕੁਦਰਤਿ ਕਵਣ ਕਹਾ ਵੀਚਾਰੁ ॥
ਵਾਰਿਆ ਨ ਜਾਵਾ ਏਕ ਵਾਰ ॥
ਜੋ ਤੁਧੁ ਭਾਵੈ ਸਾਈ ਭਲੀ ਕਾਰ ॥
ਤੂ ਸਦਾ ਸਲਾਮਤਿ ਨਿਰੰਕਾਰ ॥੧੬॥

पंच परवाण पंच परधानु ॥
पंचे पावहि दरगहि मानु ॥
पंचे सोहहि दरि राजानु ॥
पंचा का गुरु एकु धिआनु ॥
जे को कहै करै वीचारु ॥
करते कै करणै नाही सुमारु ॥
धौलु धरमु दइआ का पूतु ॥
संतोखु थापि रखिआ जिनि सूति ॥
जे को बुझै होवै सचिआरु ॥
धवलै उपरि केता भारु ॥
धरती होरु परै होरु होरु ॥
तिस ते भारु तलै कवणु जोरु ॥
जीअ जाति रंगा के नाव ॥
सभना लिखिआ वुड़ी कलाम ॥
एहु लेखा लिखि जाणै कोइ ॥
लेखा लिखिआ केता होइ ॥
केता ताणु सुआलिहु रूपु ॥
केती दाति जाणै कौणु कूतु ॥
कीता पसाउ एको कवाउ ॥
तिस ते होए लख दरीआउ ॥
कुदरति कवण कहा वीचारु ॥
वारिआ न जावा एक वार ॥
जो तुधु भावै साई भली कार ॥
तू सदा सलामति निरंकार ॥१६॥

Countless are the prayers as countless are the
  ways to perform them.
Countless are the penances as countless are the
  rituals.
Countless are the mouths that engage in reading
  and reciting the *Veda*s.
Countless are the *Yogi*s with full detachment
  reigning in their hearts.
Countless are the *Bhakta*s who revel in
  permanent ecstasy.
Countless are those who are a sacrifice unto
  humanity.
Countless are the warriors who measure their
  strength with steel.
Countless are the sages who seldom speak;
They communicate only with the Almighty.
How can I praise Thee, O Benevolent!
For, little is my power to do it.
So whatever is Thy will I bow before it.
O the Formless One! May Thou alone reign, for
  ever and ever.

ਅਸੰਖ ਜਪ ਅਸੰਖ ਭਾਉ ॥
ਅਸੰਖ ਪੂਜਾ ਅਸੰਖ ਤਪਤਾਉ ॥
ਅਸੰਖ ਗਰੰਥ ਮੁਖਿ ਵੇਦ ਪਾਠ ॥
ਅਸੰਖ ਜੋਗਾ ਮਨਿ ਰਹਹਿ ਉਦਾਸ ॥
ਅਸੰਖ ਭਗਤ ਗੁਣ ਗਿਆਨ ਵੀਚਾਰ ॥
ਅਸੰਖ ਸਤੀ ਅਸੰਖ ਦਾਤਾਰ ॥
ਅਸੰਖ ਸੂਰ ਮੁਹ ਭਖ ਸਾਰ ॥
ਅਸੰਖ ਮੋਨਿ ਲਿਵ ਲਾਇ ਤਾਰ ॥
ਕੁਦਰਤਿ ਕਵਣ ਕਹਾ ਵੀਚਾਰੁ ॥
ਵਾਰਿਆ ਨ ਜਾਵਾ ਏਕ ਵਾਰ ॥
ਜੋ ਤੁਧੁ ਭਾਵੈ ਸਾਈ ਭਲੀ ਕਾਰ ॥
ਤੂ ਸਦਾ ਸਲਾਮਤਿ ਨਿਰੰਕਾਰ ॥੧੭॥

असंख जप असंख भाउ ॥
असंख पूजा असंख तप ताउ ॥
असंख गरंथ मुखि वेद पाठ ॥
असंख जोग मनि रहहि उदास ॥
असंख भगत गुण गिआन वीचार ॥
असंख सती असंख दातार ॥
असंख सूर मुह भख सार ॥
असंख मोनि लिव लाइ तार ॥
कुदरति कवण कहा वीचारु ॥
वारिआ न जावा एक वार ॥
जो तुधु भावै साई भली कार ॥
तू सदा सलामति निरंकार ॥१७॥

Countless are the fools, stark blind.
Countless are the thieves, no better than bastards.
Countless are the kings whose conduct is full
  of tyranny.
Countless are the murderers with hands soiled
  with blood.
Countless are the sinners who sin night and day.
Countless are the liars who gloat in falsehood.
Countless are the *Maleccha*s who live on the
  polluted food.
Countless are those who live on bitching
  about others.
But the lowly Nanak asks in all humility
How come, have I not sacrificed my life
  unto you?
So, whatever is Thy will, I bow before it.
O the Formless One! May Thou reign, for ever
  and ever.

ਅਸੰਖ ਮੂਰਖ ਅੰਧ ਘੋਰ ॥
ਅਸੰਖ ਚੋਰ ਹਰਾਮਖੋਰ ॥
ਅਸੰਖ ਅਮਰ ਕਰਿ ਜਾਹਿ ਜੋਰ ॥
ਅਸੰਖ ਗਲਵਢ ਹਤਿਆ ਕਮਾਹਿ ॥
ਅਸੰਖ ਪਾਪੀ ਪਾਪੁ ਕਰਿ ਜਾਹਿ ॥
ਅਸੰਖ ਕੂੜਿਆਰ ਕੂੜੇ ਫਿਰਾਹਿ ॥
ਅਸੰਖ ਮਲੇਛ ਮਲੁ ਭਖਿ ਖਾਹਿ ॥
ਅਸੰਖ ਨਿੰਦਕ ਸਿਰਿ ਕਰਹਿ ਭਾਰੁ ॥
ਨਾਨਕੁ ਨੀਚੁ ਕਹੈ ਵੀਚਾਰੁ ॥
ਵਾਰਿਆ ਨ ਜਾਵਾ ਏਕ ਵਾਰ ॥
ਜੋ ਤੁਧੁ ਭਾਵੈ ਸਾਈ ਭਲੀ ਕਾਰ ॥
ਤੂ ਸਦਾ ਸਲਾਮਤਿ ਨਿਰੰਕਾਰ ॥੧੮॥

असंख मूरख अंध घोर ॥
असंख चोर हरामखोर ॥
असंख अमर करि जाहि जोर ॥
असंख गलवढ हतिआ कमाहि ॥
असंख पापी पापु करि जाहि ॥
असंख कूड़िआर कूड़े फिराहि ॥
असंख मलेछ मलु भखि खाहि ॥
असंख निंदक सिरि करहि भारु ॥
नानकु नीचु कहै वीचारु ॥
वारिआ न जावा एक वार ॥
जो तुधु भावै साई भली कार ॥
तू सदा सलामति निरंकार ॥१८॥

119

Countless are Thy Names and countless are Thy
    places
Unreachable are countless realms
    Thou adore
One would only be a fool who tries to count
    them
Countless are Thy manifestations
Though through words alone we give
    Thee names and praise.
Our knowledge consists of words and our
    prayers also consist of words.
Through words alone we reason, write and speak
Not just that, words alone constitute our
    relationships.
Yes, the *Nam* does not bind Thee
And whatever Thou give we receive.
Yet, the whole creation is the manifestation of the
    Nam (Divine Word).
At all places, O Nanak! Its the *Nam*
    (Divine Word) that we find.
I wonder how to praise Thy might!
Limited by nature how can I do justice to Thy
    praise, O the Unlimited One!
So, whatever is Thy will, I bow before it.
O the Formless One! May Thou reign, for ever
    and ever.

ਅਸੰਖ ਨਾਵ ਅਸੰਖ ਥਾਵ ॥
ਅਗੰਮ ਅਗੰਮ ਅਸੰਖ ਲੋਅ ॥
ਅਸੰਖ ਕਹਹਿ ਸਿਰਿ ਭਾਰੁ ਹੋਇ ॥
ਅਖਰੀ ਨਾਮੁ ਅਖਰੀ ਸਾਲਾਹ ॥
ਅਖਰੀ ਗਿਆਨੁ ਗੀਤ ਗੁਣ ਗਾਹ ॥
ਅਖਰੀ ਲਿਖਣੁ ਬੋਲਣੁ ਬਾਣਿ ॥
ਅਖਰਾ ਸਿਰਿ ਸੰਜੋਗੁ ਵਖਾਣਿ ॥
ਜਿਨਿ ਏਹਿ ਲਿਖੇ ਤਿਸੁ ਸਿਰਿ ਨਾਹਿ ॥
ਜਿਵ ਫੁਰਮਾਏ ਤਿਵ ਤਿਵ ਪਾਹਿ ॥
ਜੇਤਾ ਕੀਤਾ ਤੇਤਾ ਨਾਉ ॥
ਵਿਣੁ ਨਾਵੈ ਨਾਹੀ ਕੋ ਥਾਉ ॥
ਕੁਦਰਤਿ ਕਵਣ ਕਹਾ ਵੀਚਾਰੁ ॥
ਵਾਰਿਆ ਨ ਜਾਵਾ ਏਕ ਵਾਰ ॥
ਜੋ ਤੁਧੁ ਭਾਵੈ ਸਾਈ ਭਲੀ ਕਾਰ ॥
ਤੂ ਸਦਾ ਸਲਾਮਤਿ ਨਿਰੰਕਾਰ ॥੧੯॥

असंख नाव असंख थाव ॥
अगंम अगंम असंख लोअ ॥
असंख कहहि सिरि भारु होइ ॥
अखरी नामु अखरी सालाह ॥
अखरी गिआनु गीत गुण गाह ॥
अखरी लिखणु बोलणु बाणि ॥
अखरा सिरि संजोगु वखाणि ॥
जिनि एहि लिखे तिसु सिरि नाहि ॥
जिव फुरमाए तिव तिव पाहि ॥
जेता कीता तेता नाउ ॥
विणु नावै नाही को थाउ ॥
कुदरति कवण कहा वीचारु ॥
वारिआ न जावा एक वार ॥
जो तुधु भावै साई भली कार ॥
तू सदा सलामति निरंकार ॥१९॥

 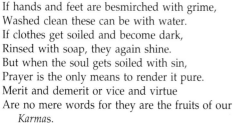

If hands and feet are besmirched with grime,
Washed clean these can be with water.
If clothes get soiled and become dark,
Rinsed with soap, they again shine.
But when the soul gets soiled with sin,
Prayer is the only means to render it pure.
Merit and demerit or vice and virtue
Are no mere words for they are the fruits of our
    *Karma*s.
Remember O Soul! As you sow so shall you reap.
Nanak! He alone decrees transmigration of
    the soul.

ਭਰੀਐ ਹਥੁ ਪੈਰੁ ਤਨੁ ਦੇਹ ॥
ਪਾਣੀ ਧੋਤੈ ਉਤਰਸੁ ਖੇਹ ॥
ਮੂਤ ਪਲੀਤੀ ਕਪੜੁ ਹੋਇ ॥
ਦੇ ਸਾਬੂਣੁ ਲਈਐ ਓਹੁ ਧੋਇ ॥
ਭਰੀਐ ਮਤਿ ਪਾਪਾ ਕੈ ਸੰਗਿ ॥
ਓਹੁ ਧੋਪੈ ਨਾਵੈ ਕੈ ਰੰਗਿ ॥
ਪੁੰਨੀ ਪਾਪੀ ਆਖਣੁ ਨਾਹਿ ॥
ਕਰਿ ਕਰਿ ਕਰਣਾ ਲਿਖਿ ਲੈ ਜਾਹੁ ॥
ਆਪੇ ਬੀਜਿ ਆਪੇ ਹੀ ਖਾਹੁ ॥
ਨਾਨਕ ਹੁਕਮੀ ਆਵਹੁ ਜਾਹੁ ॥੨੦॥

भरीऐ हथु पैरु तनु देह ॥
पाणी धोतै उतरसु खेह ॥
मूत पलीती कपडु होइ ॥
दे साबूणु लईऐ ओहु धोइ ॥
भरीऐ मति पापा कै संगि ॥
ओहु धोपै नावै कै रंगि ॥
पुंनी पापी आखणु नाहि ॥
करि करि करणा लिखि लै जाहु ॥
आपे बीजि आपे ही खाहु ॥
नानक हुकमी आवंहु जाहु ॥२०॥

Customs and rituals like pilgrimages, penances, compassion, charities, etc.
All are time-honoured practices that confer merit though not much.
However, the one who hears, sings and ruminates over the *Nam*
Goes on an inner pilgrimage that renders one pure and clean.
O God! All virtues are Thine; I have none.
Without performing good deeds to adorn, useless is Thy prayer.
Then fill your heart with the *Nam*, the muse and poesy of Lord Brahma
For, that alone shall bring out eternal truth, beauty and *ananda* (joy).
For, which was the time and which was the hour,
Which was the date and which was the day,
Which was the season and which was the month,
When the Great Lord gave shape to the Cosmos?
No Pandit did ever know it nor is it mentioned in the *Puranas* (mythology).
Nor did the Qazis know it as it finds no mention in the Quran.
No *Yogi* even knew either the day or the date;
Nor did he know the month or the season of that mighty great event.
The Creator who created the cosmos alone knows it all.
Then how can I know Him, describe Him and pray to Him?
Says Nanak: Anyway many are the pretenders who claim to know it all.
And each one is prone to making greater claims than the other.
What all, therefore, I can say is:
"Great is the Lord and great is the *Nam* which did it all."
O Nanak! Whoever says he knows it better shall only regret it in the end.

ਤੀਰਥੁ ਤਪੁ ਦਇਆ ਦਤੁ ਦਾਨੁ ॥
ਜੇ ਕੋ ਪਾਵੈ ਤਿਲ ਕਾ ਮਾਨੁ ॥
ਸੁਣਿਆ ਮੰਨਿਆ ਮਨਿ ਕੀਤਾ ਭਾਉ ॥
ਅੰਤਰਗਤਿ ਤੀਰਥਿ ਮਲਿ ਨਾਉ ॥
ਸਭਿ ਗੁਣ ਤੇਰੇ ਮੈ ਨਾਹੀ ਕੋਇ ॥
ਵਿਣੁ ਗੁਣ ਕੀਤੇ ਭਗਤਿ ਨ ਹੋਇ ॥
ਸੁਅਸਤਿ ਆਥਿ ਬਾਣੀ ਬਰਮਾਉ ॥
ਸਤਿ ਸੁਹਾਣੁ ਸਦਾ ਮਨਿ ਚਾਉ ॥
ਕਵਣੁ ਸੁ ਵੇਲਾ ਵਖਤੁ ਕਵਣੁ ਕਵਣ ਥਿਤਿ ਕਵਣੁ ਵਾਰੁ ॥
ਕਵਣਿ ਸਿ ਰੁਤੀ ਮਾਹੁ ਕਵਣੁ ਜਿਤੁ ਹੋਆ ਆਕਾਰੁ ॥
ਵੇਲ ਨ ਪਾਈਆ ਪੰਡਤੀ ਜਿ ਹੋਵੈ ਲੇਖੁ ਪੁਰਾਣੁ ॥
ਵਖਤੁ ਨ ਪਾਇਓ ਕਾਦੀਆ ਜਿ ਲਿਖਨਿ ਲੇਖੁ ਕੁਰਾਣੁ ॥
ਥਿਤਿ ਵਾਰੁ ਨਾ ਜੋਗੀ ਜਾਣੈ ਰੁਤਿ ਮਾਹੁ ਨਾ ਕੋਈ ॥
ਜਾ ਕਰਤਾ ਸਿਰਠੀ ਕਉ ਸਾਜੇ ਆਪੇ ਜਾਣੈ ਸੋਈ ॥
ਕਿਵ ਕਰਿ ਆਖਾ ਕਿਵ ਸਾਲਾਹੀ ਕਿਉ ਵਰਨੀ ਕਿਵ ਜਾਣਾ ॥
ਨਾਨਕ ਆਖਣਿ ਸਭੁ ਕੋ ਆਖੈ ਇਕ ਦੂ ਇਕੁ ਸਿਆਣਾ ॥
ਵਡਾ ਸਾਹਿਬੁ ਵਡੀ ਨਾਈ ਕੀਤਾ ਜਾ ਕਾ ਹੋਵੈ ॥
ਨਾਨਕ ਜੇ ਕੋ ਆਪੌ ਜਾਣੈ ਅਗੈ ਗਇਆ ਨ ਸੋਹੈ ॥੨੧॥

तीरथु तपु दइआ दतु दानु ॥
जे को पावै तिल का मानु ॥
सुणिआ मंनिआ मनि कीता भाउ ॥
अंतरगति तीरथि मलि नाउ ॥
सभि गुण तेरे मै नाही कोइ ॥
विणु गुण कीते भगति न होइ ॥
सुअसति आथि बाणी बरमाउ ॥
सति सुहाणु सदा मनि चाउ ॥
कवणु सु वेला वखतु कवणु कवण थिति कवणु वारु ॥
कवणि सि रुती माहु कवणु जितु होआ आकारु ॥
वेल न पाईआ पंडती जि होवै लेखु पुराणु ॥
वखतु न पाइओ कादीआ जि लिखनि लेखु कुराणु ॥
थिति वारु ना जोगी जाणै रुति माहु ना कोई ॥
जा करता सिरठी कउ साजे आपे जाणै सोई ॥
किव करि आखा किव सालाही किउ वरनी किव जाणा ॥
नानक आखणि सभु को आखै इक दू इकु सिआणा ॥
वडा साहिबु वडी नाई कीता जा का होवै ॥
नानक जे को आपौ जाणै अगै गइआ न सोहै ॥२१॥

Endless are the nether regions and endless the skies above.
Numerous were the scholars who turned weary in the quest
And reached the dead-end.
The *Veda*s tell us of many worlds above and below;
So do say the Semitic books giving the number as eighteen thousand.
But the fact is that the essence is only one.
If it could be counted someone must have done it.
The point is that all such efforts are mere vain projections.
Hence O Nanak, Great is the Lord who alone knows it all.

ਪਾਤਾਲਾ ਪਾਤਾਲ ਲਖ ਆਗਾਸਾ ਆਗਾਸ ॥
ਓੜਕ ਓੜਕ ਭਾਲਿ ਥਕੇ ਵੇਦ ਕਹਨਿ ਇਕ ਵਾਤ ॥
ਸਹਸ ਅਠਾਰਹ ਕਹਨਿ ਕਤੇਬਾ ਅਸੁਲੂ ਇਕੁ ਧਾਤੁ ॥
ਲੇਖਾ ਹੋਇ ਤ ਲਿਖੀਐ ਲੇਖੈ ਹੋਇ ਵਿਣਾਸੁ ॥
ਨਾਨਕ ਵਡਾ ਆਖੀਐ ਆਪੇ ਜਾਣੈ ਆਪੁ ॥੨੨॥

पाताला पाताल लख आगासा आगास ॥
ओड़क ओड़क भालि थके वेद कहनि इक वात ॥
सहस अठारह कहनि कतेबा असुलू इकु धातु ॥
लेखा होइ त लिखीऐ लेखै होइ विणासु ॥
नानक वडा आखीऐ आपे जाणै आपु ॥२२॥

Endless, endless were the efforts made.
But did anyone have a measure of the Lord's greatness?
For, all the rivers flow into the ocean without ever gauging its vastness.
There were kings with dominions as vast as the oceans
And wealth piled in heaps, as high as mountains.
However, they were poorer than the smallest ant,
In whose heart resides the *Nam* of the Lord.

ਸਾਲਾਹੀ ਸਾਲਾਹਿ
ਏਤੀ ਸੁਰਤਿ ਨ ਪਾਈਆ ॥
ਨਦੀਆ ਅਤੈ ਵਾਹ
ਪਵਹਿ ਸਮੁੰਦਿ ਨ ਜਾਣੀਅਹਿ ॥
ਸਮੁੰਦ ਸਾਹ ਸੁਲਤਾਨ
ਗਿਰਹਾ ਸੇਤੀ ਮਾਲੁ ਧਨੁ ॥
ਕੀੜੀ ਤੁਲਿ ਨ ਹੋਵਨੀ
ਜੇ ਤਿਸੁ ਮਨਹੁ ਨ ਵੀਸਰਹਿ ॥੨੩॥

सालाही सालाहि
एती सुरति न पाईआ ॥
नदीआ अतै वाह
पवहि समुंदि न जाणीअहि ॥
समुंद साह सुलतान
गिरहा सेती मालु धनु ॥
कीड़ी तुलि न होवनी
जे तिसु मनहु न वीसरहि ॥२३॥

Infinite is His goodness and infinite His greatness.
Infinite is His creation and infinite His munificence.
Infinite is what we see and infinite what we hear.
Even those with fertile imagination cannot measure His infinitude.
Infinite is the expanse and infinite the size.
Infinite is His measure from end to end.
However we break our heads to know Him
We cannot but fail in the endeavour.
The long and short of is that none can know the infinite He.
The more we may try, the more will it grow.
Infinite is His Eminence and infinitely exalted are His place and Name.
He alone could know His stature if he were of the same height.
But no, as none is anywhere equal to Him, He alone is His own measure
O Nanak! While His bounty is His grace,
His grace is the gift that we cherish.

ਅੰਤੁ ਨ ਸਿਫਤੀ ਕਹਣਿ ਨ ਅੰਤੁ ॥
ਅੰਤੁ ਨ ਕਰਣੈ ਦੇਣਿ ਨ ਅੰਤੁ ॥
ਅੰਤੁ ਨ ਵੇਖਣਿ ਸੁਣਣਿ ਨ ਅੰਤੁ ॥
ਅੰਤੁ ਨ ਜਾਪੈ ਕਿਆ ਮਨਿ ਮੰਤੁ ॥
ਅੰਤੁ ਨ ਜਾਪੈ ਕੀਤਾ ਆਕਾਰੁ ॥
ਅੰਤੁ ਨ ਜਾਪੈ ਪਾਰਾਵਾਰੁ ॥
ਅੰਤ ਕਾਰਣਿ ਕੇਤੇ ਬਿਲਲਾਹਿ ॥
ਤਾ ਕੇ ਅੰਤ ਨ ਪਾਏ ਜਾਹਿ ॥
ਏਹੁ ਅੰਤੁ ਨ ਜਾਣੈ ਕੋਇ ॥
ਬਹੁਤਾ ਕਹੀਐ ਬਹੁਤਾ ਹੋਇ ॥
ਵਡਾ ਸਾਹਿਬੁ ਊਚਾ ਥਾਉ ॥
ਊਚੇ ਉਪਰਿ ਊਚਾ ਨਾਉ ॥
ਏਵਡੁ ਊਚਾ ਹੋਵੈ ਕੋਇ ॥
ਤਿਸੁ ਊਚੇ ਕਉ ਜਾਣੈ ਸੋਇ ॥
ਜੇਵਡੁ ਆਪਿ ਜਾਣੈ ਆਪਿ ਆਪਿ ॥
ਨਾਨਕ ਨਦਰੀ ਕਰਮੀ ਦਾਤਿ ॥੨੪॥

अंतु न सिफती कहणि न अंतु ॥
अंतु न करणै देणि न अंतु ॥
अंतु न वेखणि सुणणि न अंतु ॥
अंतु न जापै किआ मनि मंतु ॥
अंतु न जापै कीता आकारु ॥
अंतु न जापै पारावारु ॥
अंत कारणि केते बिललाहि ॥
ता के अंत न पाए जाहि ॥
एहु अंतु न जाणै कोइ ॥
बहुता कहीऐ बहुता होइ ॥
वडा साहिबु ऊचा थाउ ॥
ऊचे उपरि ऊचा नाउ ॥
एवडु ऊचा होवै कोइ ॥
तिसु ऊचे कउ जाणै सोइ ॥
जेवडु आपि जाणै आपि आपि ॥
नानक नदरी करमी दाति ॥२४॥

So immense is His grace that it is beyond words.
But the beauty is that the Great Giver does not expect
Even a seed in return.
Even the high and mighty beg at his door.
In fact, those who do so can never be enumerated.
Even so, the ungrateful are indeed numberless
For, shameless as they are, their appetite cannot be satiated.
However, that too does happen because Thou will it thus.
If Thou will it, only then the mortal bonds are snapped.
But many are the fools that argue otherwise.
However does anyone else matter? No, Not.
And the ones who with gratitude receive His Grace
Nanak! They are the kings of kings.

ਬਹੁਤਾ ਕਰਮੁ ਲਿਖਿਆ ਨਾ ਜਾਇ ॥
ਵਡਾ ਦਾਤਾ ਤਿਲੁ ਨ ਤਮਾਇ ॥
ਕੇਤੇ ਮੰਗਹਿ ਜੋਧ ਅਪਾਰ ॥
ਕੇਤਿਆ ਗਣਤ ਨਹੀ ਵੀਚਾਰੁ ॥
ਕੇਤੇ ਖਪਿ ਤੁਟਹਿ ਵੇਕਾਰ ॥
ਕੇਤੇ ਲੈ ਲੈ ਮੁਕਰੁ ਪਾਹਿ ॥
ਕੇਤੇ ਮੂਰਖ ਖਾਹੀ ਖਾਹਿ ॥
ਕੇਤਿਆ ਦੂਖ ਭੂਖ ਸਦ ਮਾਰ ॥
ਏਹਿ ਭਿ ਦਾਤਿ ਤੇਰੀ ਦਾਤਾਰ ॥
ਬੰਦਿ ਖਲਾਸੀ ਭਾਣੈ ਹੋਇ ॥
ਹੋਰੁ ਆਖਿ ਨ ਸਕੈ ਕੋਇ ॥
ਜੇ ਕੋ ਖਾਇਕੁ ਆਖਣਿ ਪਾਇ ॥
ਓਹੁ ਜਾਣੈ ਜੇਤੀਆ ਮੁਹਿ ਖਾਇ ॥
ਆਪੇ ਜਾਣੈ ਆਪੇ ਦੇਇ ॥
ਆਖਹਿ ਸਿ ਭਿ ਕੇਈ ਕੇਇ ॥
ਜਿਸ ਨੋ ਬਖਸੇ ਸਿਫਤਿ ਸਾਲਾਹ ॥
ਨਾਨਕ ਪਾਤਿਸਾਹੀ ਪਾਤਿਸਾਹੁ ॥੨੫॥

बहुता करमु लिखिआ ना जाइ ॥
वडा दाता तिलु न तमाइ ॥
केते मंगहि जोध अपार ॥
केतिआ गणत नही वीचारु ॥
केते खपि तुटहि वेकार ॥
केते लै लै मुकरु पाहि ॥
केते मूरख खाही खाहि ॥
केतिआ दूख भूख सद मार ॥
एहि भि दाति तेरी दातार ॥
बंदि खलासी भाणै होइ ॥
होरु आखि न सके कोइ ॥
जे को खाइकु आखणि पाइ ॥
ओहु जाणै जेतीआ मुहि खाइ ॥
आपे जाणै आपे देइ ॥
आखहि सि भि केई केइ ॥
जिस नो बखसे सिफति सालाह ॥
नानक पातिसाही पातिसाहु ॥२५॥

Unexcelled are His qualities and priceless are His gifts.

Countless are His worshippers and endless are His bounties.

Priceless is that which flows in and priceless is that which goes out.

Unquestioned are His laws as unquestioned is His justice.

Perfect is His law of *Dharma* and perfect its administration

Also perfect are the weights and measures He uses for His transactions.

Priceless is His bounty and immaculate are the omens that attend upon it.

Invaluable are the points of dispensation of His grace.

Thus speak all the *Vedas* and *Puranas*;

Thus talk even the illiterate who become learned through His grace.

That's what gods like Brahma and Indra say.

That's what Krishna and His *Gopis* also uphold.

That's what the *Siddhas* and *Buddhas* do proclaim.

That's what both the gods and demons stand for.

That's what heavenly men as also saints and sages too discourse.

Yet howsoever, all combined do their best,

They fail to describe Him in all His majesty and grandeur.

Even if He Himself had thus willed,

Many more that He would have created would have failed to do it.

For, says Nanak: He is as great as His pleasure.

In fact, He alone is His measure.

That's why whoever thinks He can describes Him Is the worst among the fools of the world.

ਅਮੁਲ ਗੁਣ ਅਮੁਲ ਵਾਪਾਰ ॥
ਅਮੁਲ ਵਾਪਾਰੀਏ ਅਮੁਲ ਭੰਡਾਰ ॥
ਅਮੁਲ ਆਵਹਿ ਅਮੁਲ ਲੈ ਜਾਹਿ ॥
ਅਮੁਲ ਭਾਇ ਅਮੁਲਾ ਸਮਾਹਿ ॥
ਅਮੁਲੁ ਧਰਮੁ ਅਮੁਲੁ ਦੀਬਾਣੁ ॥
ਅਮੁਲੁ ਤੁਲੁ ਅਮੁਲੁ ਪਰਵਾਣੁ ॥
ਅਮੁਲੁ ਬਖਸੀਸ ਅਮੁਲੁ ਨੀਸਾਣੁ ॥
ਅਮੁਲੁ ਕਰਮੁ ਅਮੁਲੁ ਫੁਰਮਾਣੁ ॥
ਅਮੁਲੋ ਅਮੁਲੁ ਆਖਿਆ ਨ ਜਾਇ ॥
ਆਖਿ ਆਖਿ ਰਹੇ ਲਿਵ ਲਾਇ ॥
ਆਖਹਿ ਵੇਦ ਪਾਠ ਪੁਰਾਣ ॥
ਆਖਹਿ ਪੜੇ ਕਰਹਿ ਵਖਿਆਣ ॥
ਆਖਹਿ ਬਰਮੇ ਆਖਹਿ ਇੰਦ ॥
ਆਖਹਿ ਗੋਪੀ ਤੈ ਗੋਵਿੰਦ ॥
ਆਖਹਿ ਈਸਰ ਆਖਹਿ ਸਿਧ ॥
ਆਖਹਿ ਕੇਤੇ ਕੀਤੇ ਬੁਧ ॥
ਆਖਹਿ ਦਾਨਵ ਆਖਹਿ ਦੇਵ ॥
ਆਖਹਿ ਸੁਰਿ ਨਰ ਮੁਨਿ ਜਨ ਸੇਵ ॥
ਕੇਤੇ ਆਖਹਿ ਆਖਣਿ ਪਾਹਿ ॥
ਕੇਤੇ ਕਹਿ ਕਹਿ ਉਠਿ ਉਠਿ ਜਾਹਿ ॥
ਏਤੇ ਕੀਤੇ ਹੋਰਿ ਕਰੇਹਿ ॥
ਤਾ ਆਖਿ ਨ ਸਕਹਿ ਕੇਈ ਕੇਇ ॥
ਜੇਵਡੁ ਭਾਵੈ ਤੇਵਡੁ ਹੋਇ ॥
ਨਾਨਕ ਜਾਣੈ ਸਾਚਾ ਸੋਇ ॥
ਜੇ ਕੋ ਆਖੈ ਬੋਲੁ ਵਿਗਾੜੁ ॥
ਤਾ ਲਿਖੀਐ
ਸਿਰਿ ਗਾਵਾਰਾ ਗਾਵਾਰੁ ॥੨੬॥

अमुल गुण अमुल वापार ॥
अमुल वापारीए अमुल भंडार ॥
अमुल आवहि अमुल लै जाहि ॥
अमुल भाइ अमुला समाहि ॥
अमुलु धरमु अमुलु दीबाणु ॥
अमुलु तुलु अमुलु परवाणु ॥
अमुलु बखसीस अमुलु नीसाणु ॥
अमुलु करमु अमुलु फुरमाणु ॥
अमुलो अमुलु आखिआ न जाइ ॥
आखि आखि रहे लिव लाइ ॥
आखहि वेद पाठ पुराण ॥
आखहि पड़े करहि वखिआण ॥
आखहि बरमे आखहि इंद ॥
आखहि गोपी तै गोविंद ॥
आखहि ईसर आखहि सिध ॥
आखहि केते कीते बुध ॥
आखहि दानव आखहि देव ॥
आखहि सुरि नर मुनि जन सेव ॥
केते आखहि आखणि पाहि ॥
केते कहि कहि उठि उठि जाहि ॥
एते कीते होरि करेहि ॥
ता आखि न सकहि केई केइ ॥
जेवडु भावै तेवडु होइ ॥
नानक जाणै साचा सोइ ॥
जे को आखै बोलुविगाडु ॥
ता लिखीए
सिरि गावारा गावारु ॥२६॥

Pauri Twenty-seven
(SODAR)

Where is the wondrous door of Thy mansion, O Lord?

Seated behind which Thou watch the majesty of Thy creation?

And where always rises the sound of heavenly melodies,

Innumerable heavenly songsters playing on their instruments

Creating a veritable riot of divine symphonies;

Where eternal breezes blow and crystal waters run;

Where Dharmaraja, the king of divine justice sits in state,

ਸੋ ਦਰੁ ਕੇਹਾ ਸੋ ਘਰੁ ਕੇਹਾ
ਜਿਤੁ ਬਹਿ ਸਰਬ ਸਮਾਲੇ ॥
ਵਾਜੇ ਨਾਦ ਅਨੇਕ ਅਸੰਖਾ
ਕੇਤੇ ਵਾਵਣਹਾਰੇ ॥
ਕੇਤੇ ਰਾਗ ਪਰੀ ਸਿਉ ਕਹੀਅਨਿ
ਕੇਤੇ ਗਾਵਣਹਾਰੇ ॥
ਗਾਵਹਿ ਤੁਹਨੋ ਪਉਣੁ ਪਾਣੀ ਬੈਸੰਤਰੁ
ਗਾਵੈ ਰਾਜਾ ਧਰਮੁ ਦੁਆਰੇ ॥
ਗਾਵਹਿ ਚਿਤੁ ਗੁਪਤੁ ਲਿਖਿ ਜਾਣਹਿ
ਲਿਖਿ ਲਿਖਿ ਧਰਮੁ ਵੀਚਾਰੇ ॥
ਗਾਵਹਿ ਈਸਰੁ ਬਰਮਾ ਦੇਵੀ
ਸੋਹਨਿ ਸਦਾ ਸਵਾਰੇ ॥
ਗਾਵਹਿ ਇੰਦ ਇੰਦਾਸਣਿ ਬੈਠੇ
ਦੇਵਤਿਆ ਦਰਿ ਨਾਲੇ ॥

सो दरु केहा सो घरु केहा
जितु बहि सरब समाले ॥
वाजे नाद अनेक असंखा
केते वावणहारे ॥
केते राग परी सिउ कहीअनि
केते गावणहारे ॥
गावहि तुहनो पउणु पाणी बैसंतरु
गावै राजा धरमु दुआरे ॥
गावहि चितु गुपतु लिखि जाणहि
लिखि लिखि धरमु वीचारे ॥
गावहि ईसरु बरमा देवी
सोहनि सदा सवारे ॥
गावहि इंद इदासणि बैठे
देवतिआ दरि नाले ॥

Assisted by his two recording angels weighing
    the good and bad deeds of all;
Where the gods *Iswara*, *Brahma* and the goddess
    Devi of the divine grace
All eternally sing Thy praises in their mellifluous
    voices;
Where adorned with immortality
Indra, the king of gods, seated on
    His throne with hosts of his angels,
Never falters in singing praises at
    Thy door . . .
Where the *Siddhas* and *Buddhas* sit in supplication
    in their *Samadhis*
And where the fearless warriors and selfless
    Pandits
Add to the divine crescendo of musical voices.
And where the divine enchantresses of heart sing
    and dance with gusto.
Not just that, where gems and jewels of Thy
    creation lend colour to the scene.
And where sixty-eight sacred pools and the four
    sources of production sing
    Thy praises.
And where our cosmos and many other universes
    sing Thy praises.
Only those that Thou love can recite
    Thy *Nam*.
In no way Nanak, do I know them, nor can
    I ever recall . . .
Only Thy devotees imbued with Thy love
    adore Thou
And it happens when Thou shower
    Thy grace on them, O Master.
They behold Thy handiwork, the whole creation,
    with gratitude.
As Thou will so Thou ordain.
Whatever pleases Thou, O gracious creator,
    Thou do.
There's none who can order Thee to do anything.
Says Nanak! Thou alone are the king of kings
As Thou decree, so shall we live.

ਗਾਵਹਿ ਸਿਧ ਸਮਾਧੀ ਅੰਦਰਿ
ਗਾਵਨਿ ਸਾਧ ਵਿਚਾਰੇ ॥
ਗਾਵਨਿ ਜਤੀ ਸਤੀ ਸੰਤੋਖੀ
ਗਾਵਹਿ ਵੀਰ ਕਰਾਰੇ ॥
ਗਾਵਨਿ ਪੰਡਿਤ ਪੜਨਿ ਰਖੀਸਰ
ਜੁਗੁ ਜੁਗੁ ਵੇਦਾ ਨਾਲੇ ॥
ਗਾਵਹਿ ਮੋਹਣੀਆ ਮਨੁ ਮੋਹਨਿ
ਸੁਰਗਾ ਮਛ ਪਇਆਲੇ ॥
ਗਾਵਨਿ ਰਤਨ ਉਪਾਏ ਤੇਰੇ
ਅਠਸਠਿ ਤੀਰਥ ਨਾਲੇ ॥
ਗਾਵਹਿ ਜੋਧ ਮਹਾ ਬਲ ਸੂਰਾ
ਗਾਵਹਿ ਖਾਣੀ ਚਾਰੇ ॥
ਗਾਵਹਿ ਖੰਡ ਮੰਡਲ ਵਰਭੰਡਾ
ਕਰਿ ਕਰਿ ਰਖੇ ਧਾਰੇ ॥
ਸੇਈ ਤੁਧੁਨੋ ਗਾਵਹਿ ਜੋ ਤੁਧੁ ਭਾਵਨਿ
ਰਤੇ ਤੇਰੇ ਭਗਤ ਰਸਾਲੇ ॥
ਹੋਰਿ ਕੇਤੇ ਗਾਵਨਿ
ਸੇ ਮੈ ਚਿਤਿ ਨ ਆਵਨਿ
ਨਾਨਕੁ ਕਿਆ ਵੀਚਾਰੇ ॥
ਸੋਈ ਸੋਈ ਸਦਾ ਸਚੁ ਸਾਹਿਬੁ
ਸਾਚਾ ਸਾਚੀ ਨਾਈ ॥
ਹੈ ਭੀ ਹੋਸੀ ਜਾਇ ਨ ਜਾਸੀ
ਰਚਨਾ ਜਿਨਿ ਰਚਾਈ ॥
ਰੰਗੀ ਰੰਗੀ ਭਾਤੀ ਕਰਿ ਕਰਿ ਜਿਨਸੀ
ਮਾਇਆ ਜਿਨਿ ਉਪਾਈ ॥
ਕਰਿ ਕਰਿ ਵੇਖੈ ਕੀਤਾ ਆਪਣਾ
ਜਿਵ ਤਿਸ ਦੀ ਵਡਿਆਈ ॥
ਜੋ ਤਿਸ ਭਾਵੈ ਸੋਈ ਕਰਸੀ
ਹੁਕਮੁ ਨ ਕਰਣਾ ਜਾਈ ॥
ਸੋ ਪਾਤਿਸਾਹੁ ਸਾਹਾ ਪਾਤਿਸਾਹਿਬੁ
ਨਾਨਕ ਰਹਣੁ ਰਜਾਈ ॥੨੭॥

गावहि सिध समाधी अंदरि
गावनि साध विचारे ॥
गावनि जती सती संतोखी
गावहि वीर करारे ॥
गावनि पंडित पड़नि रखीसर
जुगु जुगु वेदा नाले ॥
गावहि मोहणीआ मनु मोहनि
सुरगा मछ पइआले ॥
गावनि रतन उपाए तेरे
अठसठि तीरथ नाले ॥
गावहि जोध महाबल सूरा
गावहि खाणी चारे ॥
गावहि खंड मंडल वरभंडा
करि करि रखे धारे ॥
सेई तुधुनो गावहि जो तुधु भावनि
रते तेरे भगत रसाले ॥
होरि केते गावनि
से मै चिति न आवनि
नानकु किआ वीचारे ॥
सोई सोई सदा सचु साहिबु
साचा साची नाई ॥
है भी होसी जाइ न जासी
रचना जिनि रचाई ॥
रंगी रंगी भाती करि करि जिनसी
माइआ जिनि उपाई ॥
करि करि वेखै कीता आपणा
जिव तिस दी वडिआई ॥
जो तिसु भावै सोई करसी
हुकमु न करणा जाई ॥
सो पातिसाहु साहा पातिसाहिबु
नानक रहणु रजाई ॥२७॥

ꙮ *Pauri* Twenty-eight ꙮ

Fill yourself with contentment in spreading your
    begging bowl, O Devotee!
And attain one-pointed mind through
    concentration.
Thus go into the world like a begging
    mendicant —
With rings of modesty in the ears and staff of
    faith in the hand.
Keep your mind and body virginally chaste
    and pure.
Do not let the roaming fancy run riot
    with you.
For, in the conquest of mind lies the conquest of
    the world.
Always remember that the Lord alone is primal
    and pure,
Without beginning and without end,
In single changeless form ever and ever.
Therefore, seek permanent refuge in
    Him only.

ਮੁੰਦਾ ਸੰਤੋਖੁ ਸਰਮੁ ਪਤੁ ਝੋਲੀ
ਧਿਆਨ ਕੀ ਕਰਹਿ ਬਿਭੂਤਿ ॥
ਖਿੰਥਾ ਕਾਲੁ ਕੁਆਰੀ ਕਾਇਆ
ਜੁਗਤਿ ਡੰਡਾ ਪਰਤੀਤਿ ॥
ਆਈ ਪੰਥੀ ਸਗਲ ਜਮਾਤੀ
ਮਨਿ ਜੀਤੈ ਜਗੁ ਜੀਤੁ ॥
ਆਦੇਸੁ ਤਿਸੈ ਆਦੇਸੁ ॥
ਆਦਿ ਅਨੀਲੁ ਅਨਾਦਿ ਅਨਾਹਤਿ
ਜੁਗੁ ਜੁਗੁ ਏਕੋ ਵੇਸੁ ॥੨੮॥

मुंदा संतोखु सरमु पतु झोली
धिआन की करहि बिभूति ॥
खिंथा कालु कुआरी काइआ
जुगति डंडा परतीति ॥
आई पंथी सगल जमाती
मनि जीतै जगु जीतु ॥
आदेसु तिसै आदेसु ॥
आदि अनीलु अनादि अनाहति
जुगु जुगु एको वेसु ॥२८॥

124

With experience of knowledge and store of
compassion
The original sound reverberates in the voids of
the world.
He, the Lord, looks after common weal and
prosperity.
Through meeting and separation does
He regulate the destiny of men.
His will is the order and hence salutations
to Him.
Always remember that the Lord alone is primal
and pure,
Without beginning and without end,
In single, changeless form ever and ever
Therefore, seek permanent refuge in Him only.

ਭੁਗਤਿ ਗਿਆਨ ਦਇਆ ਭੰਡਾਰਣਿ
ਘਟਿ ਘਟਿ ਵਾਜਹਿ ਨਾਦ ॥
ਆਪਿ ਨਾਥੁ ਨਾਥੀ ਸਭ ਜਾ ਕੀ
ਰਿਧਿ ਸਿਧਿ ਅਵਰਾ ਸਾਦ ॥
ਸੰਜੋਗੁ ਵਿਜੋਗੁ ਦੁਇ ਕਾਰ ਚਲਾਵਹਿ
ਲੇਖੇ ਆਵਹਿ ਭਾਗ ॥
ਆਦੇਸੁ ਤਿਸੈ ਆਦੇਸੁ ॥
ਆਦਿ ਅਨੀਲੁ ਅਨਾਦਿ ਅਨਾਹਤਿ
ਜੁਗੁ ਜੁਗੁ ਏਕੋ ਵੇਸੁ ॥੨੯॥

भुगति गिआनु दइआ भंडारणि
घटि घटि वाजहि नाद ॥
आपि नाथु नाथी सभ जा की
रिधि सिधि अवरा साद ॥
संजोगु विजोगु दुइ कार चलावहि
लेखे आवहि भाग ॥
आदेसु तिसै आदेसु ॥
आदि अनीलु अनादि अनाहति
जुगु जुगु एको वेसु ॥੨੯॥

It was *Maya*, the mythical Goddess who wedded
Purusha
To bear the three mighty sons, universally
accepted.
The One created the world, the Second looked
after its sustenance
And the third became Lord of the Death.
But it was God alone that made them work as
per His supreme will.
Them He saw but He Himself remained unseen.
What a great wonder! Hence, salutations to Him.
Always remember that the Lord alone is primal
and pure,
Without beginning and without end,
In single, changeless form ever and ever.
Therefore, seek permanent refuge in Him only.

ਏਕਾ ਮਾਈ ਜੁਗਤਿ ਵਿਆਈ
ਤਿਨਿ ਚੇਲੇ ਪਰਵਾਣੁ ॥
ਇਕੁ ਸੰਸਾਰੀ ਇਕੁ ਭੰਡਾਰੀ
ਇਕੁ ਲਾਏ ਦੀਬਾਣੁ ॥
ਜਿਵ ਤਿਸੁ ਭਾਵੈ ਤਿਵੈ ਚਲਾਵੈ
ਜਿਵ ਹੋਵੈ ਫੁਰਮਾਣੁ ॥
ਓਹੁ ਵੇਖੈ ਓਨਾ ਨਦਰਿ ਨ ਆਵੈ
ਬਹੁਤਾ ਏਹੁ ਵਿਡਾਣੁ ॥
ਆਦੇਸੁ ਤਿਸੈ ਆਦੇਸੁ ॥
ਆਦਿ ਅਨੀਲੁ ਅਨਾਦਿ ਅਨਾਹਤਿ
ਜੁਗੁ ਜੁਗੁ ਏਕੋ ਵੇਸੁ ॥੩੦॥

एका माई जुगति विआई
तिनि चेले परवाणु ॥
इकु संसारी इकु भंडारी
इकु लाए दीबाणु ॥
जिव तिसु भावै तिवै चलावै
जिव होवै फुरमाणु ॥
ओहु वेखै ओना नदरि न आवै
बहुता एहु विडाणु ॥
आदेसु तिसै आदेसु ॥
आदि अनीलु अनादि अनाहति
जुगु जुगु एको वेसु ॥੩੦॥

In every place He has his seat, in every place His
bountiful store.
Whatever He gives is by way of His grace.
Thus the Creator enjoys His creation.
Nanak! True is His creation as true is He Himself.
Hence salutations to Him.
He alone is primal and pure, without beginning
and without end.
In single changeless form ever and ever
Therefore seek permanent refuge in Him only.

ਆਸਣੁ ਲੋਇ ਲੋਇ ਭੰਡਾਰ ॥
ਜੋ ਕਿਛੁ ਪਾਇਆ ਸੁ ਏਕਾ ਵਾਰ ॥
ਕਰਿ ਕਰਿ ਵੇਖੈ ਸਿਰਜਣਹਾਰੁ ॥
ਨਾਨਕ ਸਚੇ ਕੀ ਸਾਚੀ ਕਾਰ ॥
ਆਦੇਸੁ ਤਿਸੈ ਆਦੇਸੁ ॥
ਆਦਿ ਅਨੀਲੁ ਅਨਾਦਿ ਅਨਾਹਤਿ
ਜੁਗੁ ਜੁਗੁ ਏਕੋ ਵੇਸੁ ॥੩੧॥

आसणु लोइ लोइ भंडार ॥
जो किछु पाइआ सु एका वार ॥
करि करि वेखै सिरजणहारु ॥
नानक सचे की साची कार ॥
आदेसु तिसै आदेसु ॥
आदि अनीलु अनादि अनाहति
जुगु जुगु एको वेसु ॥੩੧॥

Pauri Thirty-two

Even if I have a hundred thousand tongues,
multiplied twenty times
Each time I am asked each time shall
I proclaim: "The Lord of the world in One."
It is the staircase-path. Thus, ascend stairs to the
Lord's mansion, one by one.
With Him be joined in unison, listening to the
heavenly melodies.
Humility is the key to reaching His door.
Through His Grace are we guided; the rest is all
irrelevant prattle.

ਇਕ ਦੂ ਜੀਭੌ ਲਖ ਹੋਹਿ
ਲਖ ਹੋਵਹਿ ਲਖ ਵੀਸ ॥
ਲਖ ਲਖ ਗੇੜਾ ਆਖੀਅਹਿ
ਏਕੁ ਨਾਮੁ ਜਗਦੀਸ ॥
ਏਤੁ ਰਾਹਿ ਪਤਿ ਪਵੜੀਆ
ਚੜੀਐ ਹੋਇ ਇਕੀਸ ॥
ਸੁਣਿ ਗਲਾ ਆਕਾਸ ਕੀ
ਕੀਟਾ ਆਈ ਰੀਸ ॥
ਨਾਨਕ ਨਦਰੀ ਪਾਈਐ
ਕੂੜੀ ਕੂੜੈ ਠੀਸ ॥੩੨॥

इक दू जीभौ लख होहि
लख होवहि लख वीस ॥
लखु लखु गेड़ा आखीअहि
एकु नामु जगदीस ॥
एतु राहि पति पवड़ीआ
चड़ीऐ होइ इकीस ॥
सुणि गला आकास की
कीटा आई रीस ॥
नानक नदरी पाईऐ
कूड़ी कूड़ै ठीस ॥३२॥

Paurri Thirty-three

No power do we have to speak either with
eloquence or remain silent.
No power do we have to give or take.
No power do we have on life or on death.
No power do we have to gain status or lose
position.
No power do we have to immerse our mind in
thought or reason.
If anyone boasts otherwise let him try and see for
himself.
In fact, O Nanak! There is no high or low.

ਆਖਣਿ ਜੋਰੁ ਚੁਪੈ ਨਹ ਜੋਰੁ ॥
ਜੋਰੁ ਨ ਮੰਗਣਿ ਦੇਣਿ ਨ ਜੋਰੁ ॥
ਜੋਰੁ ਨ ਜੀਵਣਿ ਮਰਣਿ ਨਹ ਜੋਰੁ ॥
ਜੋਰੁ ਨ ਰਾਜਿ ਮਾਲਿ ਮਨਿ ਸੋਰੁ ॥
ਜੋਰੁ ਨ ਸੁਰਤੀ ਗਿਆਨਿ ਵੀਚਾਰਿ ॥
ਜੋਰੁ ਨ ਜੁਗਤੀ ਛੁਟੈ ਸੰਸਾਰੁ ॥
ਜਿਸੁ ਹਥਿ ਜੋਰੁ ਕਰਿ ਵੇਖੈ ਸੋਇ ॥
ਨਾਨਕ ਉਤਮੁ ਨੀਚੁ ਨ ਕੋਇ ॥੩੩॥

आखणि जोरु चुपै नह जोरु ॥
जोरु न मंगणि देणि न जोरु ॥
जोरु न जीवणि मरणि नह जोरु ॥
जोरु न राजि मालि मनि सोरु ॥
जोरु न सुरती गिआनि वीचारि ॥
जोरु न जुगती छुटै संसारु ॥
जिसु हथि जोरु करि वेखै सोइ ॥
नानक उतमु नीचु न कोइ ॥३३॥

Pauri Thirty-four

He who fixed the night and the day,
Or the air or the water or the fire or the nether
world,
He also placed the earth among them to live by
Dharma.
And embellished it with a thousand different
species.
Endless are their names and forms;
He created them according to their own deeds
and thoughts.
But among them resplendent is God.
He weighs their individual Karmas and punishes
Or on His will showers His grace.
Hence. Singing His praise is the way to earn His
solicitude.

ਰਾਤੀ ਰੁਤੀ ਥਿਤੀ ਵਾਰ ॥
ਪਵਣ ਪਾਣੀ ਅਗਨੀ ਪਾਤਾਲ ॥
ਤਿਸੁ ਵਿਚਿ ਧਰਤੀ ਥਾਪਿ ਰਖੀ ਧਰਮਸਾਲ ॥
ਤਿਸੁ ਵਿਚਿ ਜੀਅ ਜੁਗਤਿ ਕੇ ਰੰਗ ॥
ਤਿਨ ਕੇ ਨਾਮ ਅਨੇਕ ਅਨੰਤ ॥
ਕਰਮੀ ਕਰਮੀ ਹੋਇ ਵੀਚਾਰੁ ॥
ਸਚਾ ਆਪਿ ਸਚਾ ਦਰਬਾਰੁ ॥
ਤਿਥੈ ਸੋਹਨਿ ਪੰਚ ਪਰਵਾਣੁ ॥
ਨਦਰੀ ਕਰਮਿ ਪਵੈ ਨੀਸਾਣੁ ॥
ਕਚ ਪਕਾਈ ਓਥੈ ਪਾਇ ॥
ਨਾਨਕ ਗਇਆ ਜਾਪੈ ਜਾਇ ॥੩੪॥

राती रुती थिती वार ॥
पवण पाणी अगनी पाताल ॥
तिसु विचि धरती थापि रखी धरम साल॥
तिसु विचि जीअ जुगति के रंग ॥
तिन के नाम अनेक अनंत ॥
करमी करमी होइ वीचारु ॥
सचा आपि सचा दरबारु ॥
तिथै सोहनि पंच परवाणु ॥
नदरी करमि पवै नीसाणु ॥
कच पकाई ओथै पाइ ॥
नानक गइआ जापै जाइ ॥३४॥

The order of the region of *Dharma* is the rule of law.

In the end of the realm of knowledge lies His compassion.

Countless are the winds, waters and fires and countless are Krishnas and Shivas.

Countless are Brahmas who create endless species with different colours and sizes.

Countless are the realms of action and fruit and countless are the discourses on life.

Countless are the moons and the suns and on countless regions they shed their light.

Countless are the saints and sages and countless are the forms of demi-gods.

Countless are the gods, and demons as countless are jewels in the ocean.

Countless are the mines and minerals as countless are the forms of speech.

Countless have been the powerful kings and countless are the atheists.

In fact, so countless is everything O Nanak! There's no end to each one's number.

ਧਰਮ ਖੰਡ ਕਾ ਏਹੋ ਧਰਮੁ ॥
ਗਿਆਨ ਖੰਡ ਕਾ ਆਖਹੁ ਕਰਮੁ ॥
ਕੇਤੇ ਪਵਣ ਪਾਣੀ ਵੈਸੰਤਰ
ਕੇਤੇ ਕਾਨ ਮਹੇਸ ॥
ਕੇਤੇ ਬਰਮੇ ਘਾੜਤਿ ਘੜੀਅਹਿ
ਰੂਪ ਰੰਗ ਕੇ ਵੇਸ ॥
ਕੇਤੀਆ ਕਰਮ ਭੂਮੀ ਮੇਰ ਕੇਤੇ
ਕੇਤੇ ਧੂ ਉਪਦੇਸ ॥
ਕੇਤੇ ਇੰਦ ਚੰਦ ਸੂਰ ਕੇਤੇ
ਕੇਤੇ ਮੰਡਲ ਦੇਸ ॥
ਕੇਤੇ ਸਿਧ ਬੁਧ ਨਾਥ ਕੇਤੇ
ਕੇਤੇ ਦੇਵੀ ਵੇਸ ॥
ਕੇਤੇ ਦੇਵ ਦਾਨਵ ਮੁਨਿ ਕੇਤੇ
ਕੇਤੇ ਰਤਨ ਸਮੁੰਦ ॥
ਕੇਤੀਆ ਖਾਣੀ ਕੇਤੀਆ ਬਾਣੀ
ਕੇਤੇ ਪਾਤ ਨਰਿੰਦ ॥
ਕੇਤੀਆ ਸੁਰਤੀ ਸੇਵਕ ਕੇਤੇ
ਨਾਨਕ ਅੰਤੁ ਨ ਅੰਤੁ ॥੩੫॥

गिआन खंड का आखहु करमु ॥
केते पवणु पाणी वैसंतर
केते कान महेस ॥
केते बरमे घाड़ति घड़ीअहि
रूप रंग के वेस ॥
केतीआ करम भूमी मेर केते
केते धू उपदेस ॥
केते इंद चंद सूर केते
केते मंडल देस ॥
केते सिध बुध नाथ केते
केते देवी वेस ॥
केते देव दानव मुनि केते
केते रतन समुंद ॥
केतीआ खाणी केतीआ बाणी
केते पात नरिंद ॥
केतीआ सुरती सेवक केते
नानक अंतु न अंतु ॥੩੫॥

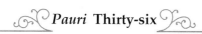

In the region of knowledge, there is no end to knowledge itself.

In this region reside myriad forms of sound, entertainment and joy.

It is the region of artistic expression, aesthetics and creative speech.

And with their help is fashioned beauty and loveliness no end,

Stupefied with which one may be rendered truly speechless.

For, anyone who attempts to define them explicitly only repents in the end.

This is the region where one can see many an achievements

Of mind and reason, science and art.

ਗਿਆਨ ਖੰਡ ਮਹਿ ਗਿਆਨੁ ਪਰਚੰਡੁ ॥
ਤਿਥੈ ਨਾਦ ਬਿਨੋਦ ਕੋਡ ਅਨੰਦੁ ॥
ਸਰਮ ਖੰਡ ਕੀ ਬਾਣੀ ਰੂਪੁ ॥
ਤਿਥੈ ਘਾੜਤਿ ਘੜੀਐ ਬਹੁਤੁ ਅਨੂਪੁ ॥
ਤਾ ਕੀਆ ਗਲਾ ਕਥੀਆ ਨਾ ਜਾਹਿ ॥
ਜੇ ਕੋ ਕਹੈ ਪਿਛੈ ਪਛੁਤਾਇ ॥
ਤਿਥੈ ਘੜੀਐ ਸੁਰਤਿ ਮਤਿ ਮਨਿ ਬੁਧਿ ॥
ਤਿਥੈ ਘੜੀਐ ਸੁਰਾ ਸਿਧਾ ਕੀ ਸੁਧਿ ॥੩੬॥

गिआन खंड महि गिआनु परचंडु ॥
तिथै नाद बिनोद कोड अनंदु ॥
सरम खंड की बाणी रूपु ॥
तिथै घाड़ति घड़ीऐ बहुतु अनूपु ॥
ता कीआ गला कथीआ ना जाहि ॥
जे को कहै पिछै पछुताइ ॥
तिथै घड़ीऐ सुरति मति मनि बुधि ॥
तिथै घड़ीऐ सुरा सिधा की सुधि ॥੩੬॥

In the region of action, triumphant are faith and sense of surrender.

Hence, there is little room for anything else.

For, therein live doughty warriors as filled with utmost valour.

In fact, in the hearts of these warriors resides God Himself.

Therein also live chaste and celestial women

Whose beauty cannot be captured in words

And who continually sing the praises of God.

Immortal as they are, they cannot be beguiled

For God Himself lives in their heart.

ਕਰਮ ਖੰਡ ਕੀ ਬਾਣੀ ਜੋਰੁ ॥
ਤਿਥੈ ਹੋਰੁ ਨ ਕੋਈ ਹੋਰੁ ॥
ਤਿਥੈ ਜੋਧ ਮਹਾ ਬਲ ਸੂਰ ॥
ਤਿਨ ਮਹਿ ਰਾਮੁ ਰਹਿਆ ਭਰਪੂਰਿ ॥
ਤਿਥੈ ਸੀਤੋ ਸੀਤਾ ਮਹਿਮਾ ਮਾਹਿ ॥
ਤਾ ਕੇ ਰੂਪ ਨ ਕਥਨੇ ਜਾਹਿ ॥
ਨਾ ਓਹਿ ਮਰਹਿ ਨ ਠਾਗੇ ਜਾਹਿ ॥
ਜਿਨ ਕੈ ਰਾਮੁ ਵਸੈ ਮਨ ਮਾਹਿ ॥
ਤਿਥੈ ਭਗਤ ਵਸਹਿ ਕੇ ਲੋਅ ॥

करम खंड की बाणी जोरु ॥
तिथै होरु न कोई होरु ॥
तिथै जोध महाबल सूर ॥
तिन महि रामु रहिआ भरपूर ॥
तिथै सीतो सीता महिमा माहि ॥
ता के रूप न कथने जाहि ॥
ना ओहि मरहि न ठागे जाहि ॥
जिन कै रामु वसै मन माहि ॥
तिथै भगत वसहि के लोअ ॥

127

There too live the courageous soldier-saints
Whose hearts are filled with eternal bliss of
    the Formless.
Lastly, in the realm of truth (*Sach Khand*)
    lives God, the Formless Himself,
Who watches His creation with eyes full of
    compassion.
Therein shine earths, realms and spheres
And no words can ever describe their glory.
There are endless forms of life there
And each one acts according as He alone wills.
O Nanak! It is the final destination of all
But it's not possible to describe it.

ਕਰਹਿ ਅਨੰਦੁ ਸਚਾ ਮਨਿ ਸੋਇ ॥
ਸਚ ਖੰਡਿ ਵਸੈ ਨਿਰੰਕਾਰੁ ॥
ਕਰਿ ਕਰਿ ਵੇਖੈ ਨਦਰਿ ਨਿਹਾਲ ॥
ਤਿਥੈ ਖੰਡ ਮੰਡਲ ਵਰਭੰਡ ॥
ਜੇ ਕੋ ਕਥੈ ਤ ਅੰਤ ਨ ਅੰਤ ॥
ਤਿਥੈ ਲੋਅ ਲੋਅ ਆਕਾਰ ॥
ਜਿਵ ਜਿਵ ਹੁਕਮੁ ਤਿਵੈ ਤਿਵ ਕਾਰ ॥
ਵੇਖੈ ਵਿਗਸੈ ਕਰਿ ਵੀਚਾਰੁ ॥
ਨਾਨਕ ਕਥਨਾ ਕਰੜਾ ਸਾਰੁ ॥੩੭॥

करहि अनंदु सचा मनि सोइ ॥
सच खंडि वसै निरंकारु ॥
करि करि वेखै नदरि निहाल ॥
तिथै खंड मंडल वरभंड ॥
जे को कथै त अंत न अंत ॥
तिथै लोअ लोअ आकार ॥
जिव जिव हुकमु तिवै तिव कार ॥
वेखै विगसै करि वीचारु ॥
नानक कथना करड़ा सारु ॥੩੭॥

Pauri Thirty-eight

However, as we in life are required to mint the
    true coin
In the crucible of restraint
Let the goldsmith of infinite patience work
With the hammer of spiritual knowledge,
On the anvil of divinity.
Not just that. Let prayer and austerity fan
    the fire.
Then with the nectar of God's love
Lord's imprint be embossed on it,
Finally immersing it in the sacred waters.
This way is the coin of *Nam* made in the
    mint of truth.
Thus, those who are favoured with the
    grace of God
Are the recipients of His compassion.
In fact, they are, O Nanak, blessed by Him, with
    eternal joy.

ਜਤੁ ਪਾਹਾਰਾ ਧੀਰਜੁ ਸੁਨਿਆਰੁ ॥
ਅਹਰਣਿ ਮਤਿ ਵੇਦੁ ਹਥੀਆਰੁ ॥
ਭਉ ਖਲਾ ਅਗਨਿ ਤਪ ਤਾਉ ॥
ਭਾਂਡਾ ਭਾਉ ਅੰਮ੍ਰਿਤੁ ਤਿਤੁ ਢਾਲਿ ॥
ਘੜੀਐ ਸਬਦੁ ਸਚੀ ਟਕਸਾਲ ॥
ਜਿਨ ਕਉ ਨਦਰਿ ਕਰਮੁ ਤਿਨ ਕਾਰ ॥
ਨਾਨਕ ਨਦਰੀ ਨਦਰਿ ਨਿਹਾਲ ॥੩੮॥

जतु पाहारा धीरजु सुनिआरु ॥
अहरणि मति वेदु हथीआरु ॥
भउ खला अगनि तप ताउ ॥
भांडा भाउ अंम्रितु तितु ढालि ॥
घड़ीऐ सबदु सची टकसाल ॥
जिन कउ नदरि करमु तिन कार ॥
नानक नदरी नदरि निहाल ॥੩੮॥

SLOKA

The air is the guide, the water the father and the
    earth the mother.
Day and night are in the role of nurses.
And this world is the vast playground
In the lap of which one play-acts his life's drama.
Acts, good and bad, are judged in the court of
    Dharmaraja
At the time of one's death.
Thus, everyone is seated near or far from You
    O Lord!
Strictly in accordance with his own deeds.
What it means is that those
Who persevere endlessly in repeating the *Nam*,
Their faces alone come out radiant;
And they are liberated from the cycle of birth
    and death.

ਪਵਣੁ ਗੁਰੂ ਪਾਣੀ ਪਿਤਾ
ਮਾਤਾ ਧਰਤਿ ਮਹਤੁ ॥
ਦਿਵਸੁ ਰਾਤਿ ਦੁਇ ਦਾਈ ਦਾਇਆ
ਖੇਲੈ ਸਗਲ ਜਗਤੁ ॥
ਚੰਗਿਆਈਆ ਬੁਰਿਆਈਆ
ਵਾਚੈ ਧਰਮੁ ਹਦੂਰਿ ॥
ਕਰਮੀ ਆਪੋ ਆਪਣੀ
ਕੇ ਨੇੜੈ ਕੇ ਦੂਰਿ ॥
ਜਿਨੀ ਨਾਮੁ ਧਿਆਇਆ
ਗਏ ਮਸਕਤਿ ਘਾਲਿ ॥
ਨਾਨਕ ਤੇ ਮੁਖ ਉਜਲੇ
ਕੇਤੀ ਛੁਟੀ ਨਾਲਿ ॥੧॥

पवणु गुरू पाणी पिता
माता धरति महतु ॥
दिवसु राति दुइ दाई दाइआ
खेलै सगल जगतु ॥
चंगिआईआ बुरिआईआ
वाचै धरमु हदूरि ॥
करमी आपो आपणी
के नेड़ै के दूरि ॥
जिनी नामु धिआइआ
गए मसकति घालि ॥
नानक ते मुख उजले
केती छुटी नालि ॥੧॥

(Rendition: Author)   *(Original Panjabi: S.G.P.C.)*   *(Devanagari Transliteration)*

Select Bibliography

Sikh Scholars

Kaur Madanjit : Guru Nanak and His Teachings (Edited 1989), GND University, Amritsar.

Singh Bhai Veer : Puratan Janam Sakhi (Edited 1948), Amritsar.

Singh Daljeet : Essentials of Sikhism (1994), Singh Brothers, Amritsar.

Singh Diwan : Revolution of Guru Nanak, People's Publishing House, Chandigarh.

Singh Doabia Harbans : Sacred Dialogues of Guru Nanak Dev. Singh Brothers, Amritsar.

Singh Harbans : Perspective on Guru Nanak (Edited Seminar Papers Commemorating the five hundredth anniversary of Nanak) (1990), Punjabi University, Patiala.

Singh Harbans : Guru Nanak, Delhi Sikh Gurdwara Management Committee, Delhi.

Singh Jagtar Grewal : Guru Nanak in History (1979), Panjab University, Chandigarh.

Singh Jagjit : The Sikh Revolution (1984), Kendri Singh Sabha, Amritsar.

Singh Khushwant : A History of the Sikhs – Two volumes (1963, 1966) , University of Princeton, USA.

Singh Puran : The Book of Ten Masters (1926), London.

Singh Raja Sir Daljit : Guru Nanak (Life, Travels, Teachings) (1943), Unity Publishers, Lahore.

Singh Ranbir : The Sikh Way of Life (1968), India Publishers, New Delhi.

Singh Rattan Jaggi : Guru Nanak Bani (1969), Punjabi University, Patiala.

Singh Sohan Seetal : Guru Nanak 1968, Language Department, Panjab, Patiala.

Singh Surjit Bal : Life of Guru Nanak (1969), Panjab University Chandigarh.

Singh Taran : Guru Nanak as a Poet (Ph. D. Thesis manuscript) Panjab University, Chandigarh.

Singh Taran : Teachings of Guru Nanak, Punjabi University, Patiala.

Singh Trilochan : Guru Nanak, Founder of Sikhism (1968), DSGM Committee, Delhi.

Singh Vidyarthi Devender : Sri Guru Nanak Abhinandan, GND University, Amritsar.

Non-Sikh Scholars

Bannerjee A.C. : Guru Nanak and His Times (1978), Punjabi University, Patiala.

Bannerji Indu Bhushan : Evolution of the Khalsa – two volumes, A. Mukherjee & Co., Calcutta.

Fani Mohsin : Dabistan-i-Mazahib (1321 AH), Nawal Kishore Press, Lucknow.

Gupta Hari Ram : History of Sikh Gurus (1952), Minerva Book Shop, Shimla.

Latif Syed Muhammad : History of Panjab (1889), Jhang (Now Pakistan).

Narang Gokul Chand : Transformation of Sikhism (1912), London, Republished by New Book Society of India, New Delhi.

Ray Niharranjan : The Sikh Gurus and the Sikh Society (1970), Punjabi University, Patiala.

Tiwari Vishwa Nath : Krantikari Guru Nanak, Panjab University, Chandigarh.

Varma Sharad Chandra : Guru Nanak and the Logos of Divine Manifestation (1969), Delhi

Non-Indian Scholars

Cunninghm J.D. : A History of the Sikhs (1849), Oxford University Press, London.

Macauliffe M.A. : The Sikh Religion, 1 to 6 volumes, Oxford University Press, London.

Mcleod W.H. : Guru Nanak and Sikh Religion (1968), Oxford University Press, London.

Scott G.B. : Religion and Short History of the Sikhs (1970), Panjab Language Department, Patiala.

Smith Vincent A. : Oxford History of India, Oxford University Press, London.

Toynbee A. : A Study of History (1971) Oxford University Press, London.

(As prepared by Prof. Dalip Singh, Mumbai)

Other Books in the Introduction Series

HINDUISM — An Introduction
Shakunthala Jagannathan

GANESHA — The Auspicious ... The Beginning
Shakunthala Jagannathan, Nanditha Krishna

BALAJI VENKATESHWARA — An Introduction
Nanditha Krishna

SHIVA — An Introduction
Devdutt Pattanaik

VISHNU — An Introduction
Devdutt Pattanaik

DEVI, *The Mother-Goddess* — An Introduction
Devdutt Pattanaik

HANUMAN — An Introduction
Devdutt Pattanaik

LAKSHMI — An Introduction
Devdutt Pattanaik